FOCUS ON THE FAMILY PRESENTS

Adventures in ODYSSEY

Candid Conversations with Connie, Vol 2

KATHY BUCHANAN

Tyndale House Publishers, Inc.
Carol Stream, Illinois

Candid Conversations with Connie, Vol. 2:
A Girl's Guide to Boys, Peer Pressure, and Cliques
© 2015 Focus on the Family

A Focus on the Family book published by
Tyndale House Publishers, Inc., Carol Stream, Illinois 60188

Focus on the Family and Adventures in Odyssey, and the accompanying logos and designs, are federally registered trademarks of Focus on the Family, 8605 Explorer Drive, Colorado Springs, CO 80920.

TYNDALE and Tyndale's quill logo are registered trademarks of Tyndale House Publishers, Inc.

All Scripture quotations, unless otherwise marked, are taken from the *Holy Bible, New International Version*®. NIV®. Copyright © 1973, 1978, 1984 by Biblica, Inc.™ Used by permission of Zondervan. All rights reserved worldwide (*www.zondervan.com*).

Scripture quotations marked (2011) are taken from the *Holy Bible, New International Version*®. NIV®. Copyright © 1973, 1978, 1984, 2011 by Biblica, Inc.™ Used by permission of Zondervan. All rights reserved worldwide (*www.zondervan.com*).

Scripture quotations marked (ESV) are taken from *The Holy Bible, English Standard Version*. Copyright © 2001 by CrosswayBibles, a publishing ministry of Good News Publishers. Used by permission. All rights reserved.

Scripture quotations marked (NLT) are taken from the *Holy Bible, New Living Translation*, copyright © 1996, 2004, 2007, 2013 by Tyndale House Foundation. Used by permission of Tyndale House Publishers, Inc., Carol Stream, Illinois 60188. All rights reserved.

The use of material from or references to various websites does not imply endorsement of those sites in their entirety. Availability of websites and pages is subject to change without notice.

No part of this publication may be reproduced, stored in a retrieval system, or transmitted in any form or by any means—electronic, mechanical, photocopy, recording, or otherwise—without prior written permission of Focus on the Family.

Cover design by Jennifer Ghionzoli
Interior design by Lexie Rhodes
Illustrations by Gary Locke

Library of Congress Cataloging-in-Publication Data for this title can be found at www.loc.gov.

ISBN: 978-1-58997-797-6

For manufacturing information regarding this product, please call 1-800-323-9400.

Printed in the United States of America
1 2 3 4 5 6 7 8 9 / 21 20 19 18 17 16 15

For my daughter, Maleah, who has taught me so much about faith, imagination, and the power of a hug. You brighten my life every single day.
—*Kathy Buchanan*

Contents

Introduction 1

Chapter One: Peppered Salami Is Underrated 3
  (Knowing Who You Are)

Chapter Two: When Penny Saved My Life 17
  (Finding Fantastic Friends)

Chapter Three: The Joys of Friendship 31
  (Gossiping, Drama Queens, and Frenemies)

Chapter Four: Get the Garlic out of Your Pudding 47
  (Learning to Lead)

Chapter Five: Crying into My Pizza 61
  (Understanding Cliques)

Chapter Six: Adventures of the Nerd Bird 73
  (How to Handle a Mean Girl)

Chapter Seven: Once upon a Yellow-and-Pink-Checkered
  Jacket 89
  (What to Do About Peer Pressure)

CONTENTS

Chapter Eight: Blame It on My Hippocampus 101
  (How to Make Good Decisions)

Chapter Nine: Tapping into Your Superpower 117
  (Skills for Surviving . . . and Thriving)

Chapter Ten: How to Survive Mad Cow Disease 131
  (The Laws of Like)

Chapter Eleven: A Knight in Shining Arrogance 143
  (How to Spot a Godly Guy)

Chapter Twelve: Brain Problems, Zip Lines, and Homeless
  Puppy Dogs 155
  (Q & A About Guys . . . with the Guys Themselves)

Appendix 167
  (Verses About How God Sees You)

Notes 169

Introduction

It all started with an argument over pickle relish.

See, my friend Penny insisted that pickle relish makes everything better: hot dogs, omelets, french fries, egg salad . . .

"Egg salad?" I said. "You can't put pickle relish in egg salad."

"Egg salad can't even be called egg salad without pickle relish," Penny said. "That's like a peanut-butter-and-jelly sandwich without the bread!"

I disagreed. Strongly.

So we decided we'd each make egg-salad sandwiches according to our tastes, take them to Whit's End, and find out which sandwich people liked better.

Olivia and Emily were sitting at the counter when we walked into the ice-cream shop. I pulled out the sandwiches.

"Are we having a picnic?" Olivia asked.

"That's a fantastic idea!" Penny said.

So we dug up some strawberry ice cream, pineapple chunks, and a can of whipped cream to round out our picnic. (There weren't a lot of options in the Whit's End kitchen.) Then we set up in McAlister Park.

Camilla came over after she finished her soccer game. Tamika had been reading under a tree and joined us too. And, well, pretty soon we had a whole crew of girls hanging out, enjoying the sunshine and pineapple chunks.

The conversation went from what's really in a can of whipped cream to which cloud looked the most like Jason Whittaker to how nerve-racking starting school next week would be for the girls.

"Why are you nervous?" asked Penny.

Well, this brought up a whole slew of answers: cliques, boys, snobs, and friends. Then more issues surfaced: *not* having friends, difficult friends, feeling awkward, being embarrassed, peer pressure, locker trouble, being made fun of, and eating cafeteria food.

"Being a teen is tough," said Olivia through a mouthful of pickle-relish-free egg-salad sandwich. (I've always liked Olivia.)

"Yeah, how did you survive it?" Tamika looked at me.

So we started talking about it. And I thought you might enjoy the conversation too!

I'm going to be sharing some of my most personal—and embarrassing—moments. Like how I got my head stuck in an owl costume, the day I called Larry Melwood a geek, and the weeks I spent crying into my pizza in the girls' locker room.

C'mon, there's room on the blanket and plenty of egg-salad sandwiches. If you stick with us enough, you'll even find out which kind of egg salad is best . . .

Chapter 1

Peppered Salami Is Underrated

(Knowing Who You Are)

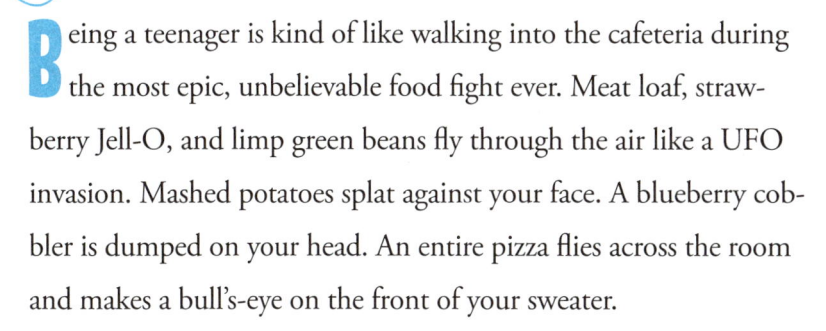

Being a teenager is kind of like walking into the cafeteria during the most epic, unbelievable food fight ever. Meat loaf, strawberry Jell-O, and limp green beans fly through the air like a UFO invasion. Mashed potatoes splat against your face. A blueberry cobbler is dumped on your head. An entire pizza flies across the room and makes a bull's-eye on the front of your sweater.

You rush from the cafeteria into the restroom. As you stand in front of the mirror, you hardly recognize yourself.

You get so covered by the concerns about what other people think, doubts about your worth, and the opinions the kids around you have about dating, fitting in, and growing up that you forget who you really are.

But here's one thing I've learned: to survive—and thrive—during these years, *you've got to know who you are.*

You've got to wash off the pressures, criticism, and embarrassing moments like that blueberry cobbler in your hair. Then live with confidence that the janitor will mop it up later. (Well . . . that's where the analogy breaks down, but you get what I mean, right?)

Tales of a Seventh-Grade Outsider

For me, seventh grade brought my first pimple, a frizzy perm, and my bizarre fear of staplers.[*] Yep, that's right . . . a fear of staplers.

Junior high was a time when I didn't really know who I was, so I tried to become what everyone else expected me to be. One of those everyones was Natalie VanUbenstein. She was running for student body president, and I volunteered to work on her campaign. I didn't know Natalie—except that she was really popular. I didn't know her plans for improving the school—except

---

[*] To hear Adventures in Odyssey audio dramas about Connie Kendall's life, visit *WhitsEnd.org*—and to find out more about this phobia, listen to "Mum's the Word," episode 602, album 47, *Into the Light.*

to add more purple, which was her favorite color. And I didn't know how to help her campaign—except to hang purple posters all over school that said, "It's the time—vote VanUbenstein!" (It really was an unfortunate name for a person seeking political office.)

I was the last student to leave school the afternoon of the poster hanging. (I wanted Natalie to be impressed with my commitment.) But as I was stapling the last poster with my heavy-duty, easy-squeeze staple gun, I accidentally stapled my thumb to a bulletin board. Ow! I jerked back to pull away, but instead I unintentionally jammed the staple-gun trigger in the "on" position. It began spitting metal like crazy—stapling my sweater, hair, and somehow even my sock to the bulletin board!

I was stapled next to the school lunch menu for forty-five minutes before a janitor finally rescued me.

You can see how this would be traumatic. To this day, even the sound of a staple gun will cause me to jump ten feet in the air and cling to a ceiling fan.

Of course, having a phobia of staplers didn't help me fit in any better at school. It only made me feel more weird—more like an outsider. Like peppered salami in a world of deli turkey. Turkey just fits in. Everyone loves it. But it's the rare person who chooses salami. Everyone else in seventh grade seemed to know the right way to be. But somehow I was ziplocked into a stay-fresh bag of cluelessness. I began to wonder, *What's wrong with me and how can I change?*

Since then, I've learned that my quirks are actually what make me "Connie." I mean, if I looked and acted and made decisions like everyone else, I wouldn't be Connie Kendall. I'd be Human Girl number 6,921,008,308 or something equally boring. But in junior high, I hated my quirks. My friends can relate:

>TAMIKA: I got orange socks before school one year, and I was superexcited to wear them. I thought they were unique and fun. Until everyone started asking me if I'd lost a dare or if I realized how ridiculous I looked. Oops!
>
>PENNY: I couldn't find my locker on the first day of junior high, so I thought, *Well, I'll just ask this nice, older girl. She'll help me out.* And she did. She gave me directions to the Dumpsters behind the gym. (I probably should have guessed the directions were wrong before I ended up outside.) Anyway, for years afterward, the upperclassmen called me Dumpster Girl. It got old. Actually, it was old as soon as they said it the first time.
>
>OLIVIA: I wore jeans and a green T-shirt on the first day of eighth grade. My hair was pulled back in a ponytail. Amber Grayson sneered when I walked by. "Why are you dressed so strange?" she said. I thought I looked pretty

normal. "Nobody dresses like that," she said and then walked away. Really?

Camilla: I felt so much pressure from other kids my age. I was trying to figure out how I was supposed to dress, look, and act. Should I wear a beret? Should I raise my hand in class? Should I talk to the girl wearing weird glasses? It seemed impossible to have it all together.

Emily: All my friends were boy-crazy and wanted to know who I liked and who I didn't like. But I didn't even care. And they were like, "What? You don't care?" And I felt like a freak.

These are *supercommon* problems: feeling peer pressure, fitting in, being made fun of, liking boys, and choosing friends. It's easy to feel like you're being attacked from all sides.

Here's a Secret...

I wear a necklace with a cross on it as a reminder that God is always with me. And that what He says about me is truer than what anyone else says. Sometimes I just rub the cross with my fingers to remind myself I'm not alone. Maybe you'd also like to go get a necklace, bracelet, or ring to wear as a reminder that God is always by your side.

When the Massive Food Fight Comes Your Way . . .

Over the next several years, you'll have a lot of things thrown at you. But getting around these dilemmas won't be as simple as dodging mashed potatoes in a food fight. You'll hear words from others (and even in your own head) telling you that you're not *enough*—not pretty enough, talented enough, cool enough, important enough. You'll wonder if you should change so a certain group of girls will accept you or so a certain boy will like you. You'll start questioning things that you know for sure now.

When all that comes at you, you must trust the truth about how God sees you. The Bible says you are His "chosen people," "a royal priesthood" and "God's special possession" (1 Peter 2:9, 2011). The knowledge of who you are in God's eyes can make it easier to choose what words to believe and who your friends should be. And then it'll be easier to make the right decisions. (Notice, I didn't say easy—just easier.)

So when someone calls you a nasty name, you'll know it's not true. *Because you'll know you're amazing.*

Or when you feel pressure to drink alcohol because that's what everyone else is doing, you'll know you don't have to. *Because you'll know what your standards are.*

And when your friends are convinced that you're nobody until you have a boyfriend, you'll be able to laugh it off. *Because you'll know you're worth more than that.*

And when everyone judges you by what you wear or weigh or how your hair looks, you'll have a better perspective. *Because you'll know what's really important.*

And when you have that terrible, horrible day that you'd like to forget, you won't forget the *right* voice to listen to. Because one day you might trip on the softball field and cost your team the game, or start crying when you're giving a speech in front of the school, or flunk that chemistry exam, and then you'll hear a couple different voices:

> Voice Number One: I'm a total loser, and I can't believe anyone would want to be my friend. No one wants me around. I just mess up all the time. I might as well hide from everyone. Who really cares what I do anyway?

Or . . .

> Voice Number Two: I messed up. I'm really disappointed in myself. I disappointed others, but that doesn't define who I am. God created me to be His daughter. I'm important and created for a purpose. God knows my whole story, and He's teaching me things. This matters. I matter. And even though I would've happily redone this day, I'm glad to be alive.

Which voice do you think God wants you to listen to?

You're entering a time when you'll likely grow up a lot—and that's something to be proud of. You'll laugh harder than you ever have. You'll find the best friends you've ever known. You'll learn new things. Discover secret talents. Recognize interests and gifts you never realized you possessed. Enjoy all the fun things coming your way . . . without letting the food fights ruin them.

Your Turn

This will be fun—really! Find an old notebook. Maybe last year's history book that's filled only halfway with notes. Or you can use the lines below. Start answering the following questions. (I asked the girls to do this, and they've shared some of their answers!)

1. *What do I believe?* This is a pretty deep question. But give it some thought. What do you believe about God and the Bible? Why do you think He created you? What's your purpose in the world?

_____

_____

_____

_____

TAMIKA: I believe that God created me for a purpose and that He has a plan for my life. I believe that God loves me and that Jesus died to forgive my sins. I want to love God by obeying what the Bible says. Being honest, caring for others, and trying to be unselfish are important. Attending church and being with my family are important to me too.

2. *What am I good at?* You don't have to be an expert, but list your talents and skills—like athletics, relationships, hobbies, or whatever. You're probably good at more things than you think. You can even ask your parents or friends for their observations.

_____

_____

_____

_____

This is what I wrote down in my journal: I'm a good writer, and I'm gifted at connecting with other people. I'm pretty friendly and outgoing. God has given me some organization and leadership skills. I'm good at encouraging others and giving them advice when they need it. I'm a decent public speaker. (Oh, and I make really delicious french toast.)

3. *What do I enjoy?* Think about things that make you happy—flavors, smells, activities—or people who make you feel really alive. You can even jot down favorite memories and moments. This is probably a list you'll add to over the years, because you'll always be finding new things you love.

_____

_____

_____

_____

_____

Olivia: I like spending time with my family, waterskiing, reading, acting, pruning lilacs, and teasing my little brother. My favorite ice cream is mint chocolate chip, and my favorite thing to do on a Saturday is go to Whit's End and try on different outfits in the costume room. I had the best time being the lead in a play Connie directed.

You may not know what you like to do at this point in your life. And that's okay, because now is your opportunity to experience new activities and find out where you fit in and shine the most! Go ahead and join the swim team and take art classes and write for the school paper. Audition for choir and the school play. Take up an instrument. Do anything that interests you. See what you enjoy. Then keep adding things to your list.

4. *List three qualities you hope people notice in you.* What are the character qualities people compliment you on? Or the things you most appreciate about yourself?

_____

_____

_____

Olivia: creative, funny, kind
Camilla: compassionate, athletic, likable
Penny: wise, artistic, unique
Tamika: adventurous, hardworking, enthusiastic
Emily: intelligent, curious, disciplined

You could use a ton more adjectives, too: Maybe you want to be known as cheerful, thoughtful, organized, friendly, imaginative, fun, strong, understanding, or brave.

5. *What are my goals?* Dream big with this. You might not know your future career—that's fine; very few teens do. (I'm *still* trying to figure out mine!) But think about things you'd like to do during your life. Have a family? Travel around the world? Go to college? Live in outer space? Cure cancer?

_____

_____

_____

_____

_____

Camilla: I want to get a soccer scholarship. Then I want to go back to Kenya to work in an orphanage for a year. My family went there last year, and the experience really made me realize what's important in life. And it's *not* having a lot of things. I think I'd like to grow up to be an animal keeper at a zoo or play on the US Olympic soccer team.

Then—and here's the *superimportant* part—learn how God sees you. Even when we don't see ourselves clearly, we can trust that God knows us better than we know ourselves. He's our FFF (Forever Father and Friend), which is way better than a BFF.

6. *What does the Bible have to say to me?* Jot down verses that have been important to you over the past few years. Take a look at the appendix on page 167. Read these verses out loud; really *think* about them. Circle all the truths where God says this is who you are! Do any of these verses stand out as ones you want to remember? If so, list them.

_____

_____

_____

_____

_____

_____

CHAPTER 2

When Penny Saved My Life

(Finding Fantastic Friends)

When I first met my best friend, Penny, she saved my life. Well, at least it felt like it. I was in this college art class, which was wa-a-ay over my head. Penny sat next to me and could tell I was nervous, so she offered to be my partner—even though she had plenty of friends in the class. She was encouraging, kind, funny, and quirky—everything you'd want in a best friend. (Well, except being involved in criminal activity . . . but that was all a big misunderstanding.)*

---

* To find out more about how Connie met Penny, listen to album 53, *The Green Ring Conspiracy*, episodes 679–690.

Before I met Penny, I went a long time without a really great friend. Sure, I had Mr. Whittaker and Eugene. But Whit was more like a dad, and Eugene was like that brilliant older brother you never fully understand. And, of course, Tom and Bernard were always fun to hang around with, but they were more like mentors in my life. I didn't have a good "let's go shopping and have a slumber party and stay up late eating cookie dough" kind of friend. And I needed one.

Friendships aren't just important to us; they were important to Jesus, too. I like to think about Jesus and His disciple buddies joking around, making memories together ("Did you see the look on that guy's face when we kept giving him more bread and fish?"), or good-naturedly teasing each other ("Got you some swimming lessons for your birthday, Peter") or having their own inside jokes ("Let's see if John is so lovable after he finds this three-day-old fish in his sleeping bag"). Jesus really got to know His friends—and they Him. The group was together constantly—traveling, eating, sleeping, arguing, laughing, talking about God, learning deep spiritual truths, telling stories. Minus the miracles, it probably would have been a lot like you hanging out with your friends.

Jesus had a personality and a sense of humor. He shared His life with a community of friends. So why would we be any different? God designed us to need other people in our lives and to have relationships with them. So the fact that you desire friendships—and a place to belong—is natural and healthy.

I asked the girls at our picnic what characteristics were important to them in a good friend. Here's what they said:

- Someone who's really honest with me. She tells me when I have chocolate pudding smudged on my nose after lunch, or when my attempt at a new hairstyle doesn't work. But she does it in a kind way—and I know it's because she loves me, not that she wants to hurt me.
- I can be totally weird and crazy around her, and she doesn't roll her eyes at me. She's weird and crazy right back.
- She prays for me when I'm worried about something, and she reminds me that God is in control—even if it doesn't feel like it.
- She likes me not just when I'm happy and helpful but also when I'm depressed and discouraged. She'll sit with me and genuinely wants to know what's wrong. I don't have to pretend to be fine if I'm not.
- She knows me inside and out. She knows my favorite milkshake flavor and what I like on my pizza. When she's on a family vacation, she'll buy me a gift (a magnet or whatever) just because she knows I'll like it. She sticks close when I have to play volleyball in gym class, just because she knows I hate it.

- When I do something completely embarrassing—like fall into the fountain at the mall because I'm too busy texting—she still claims me as a friend.
- We laugh at all the same things. We always have fun together.
- We can disagree with each other. I know she won't end our friendship just because I choose a different movie than what she wants to watch. At the same time, we accommodate each other. I'll play the game she wants to play, and we'll play my favorite game the next day.

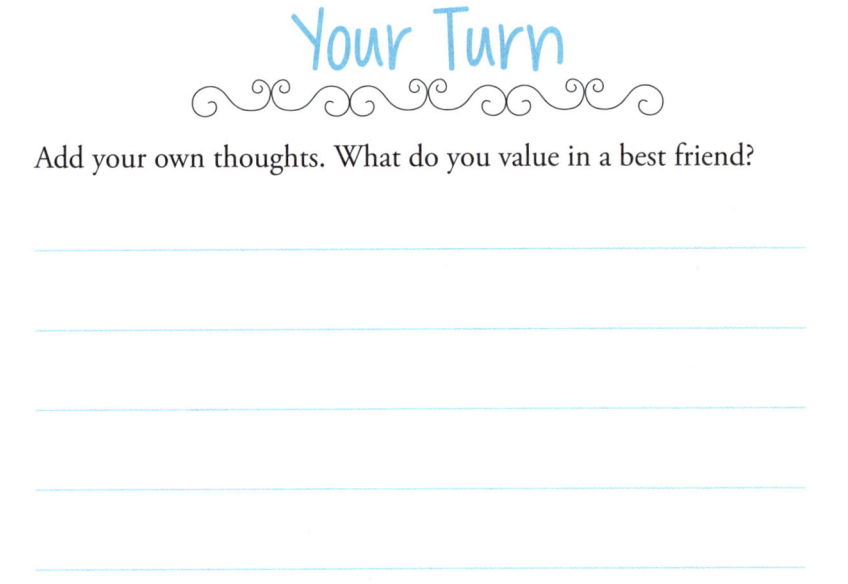

Your Turn

Add your own thoughts. What do you value in a best friend?

_____

_____

_____

_____

Are *you* that type of friend? Remember, to have (and keep) good friends, you need to *be* a good friend.

Quality Friends

Below are some qualities of a good friend. Nobody's perfect, so don't feel bad for not showing all these traits all the time. Circle the qualities that you are pretty sure you have. Then put a box around the ones you could work at a little harder. Maybe ask a friend to help you out by giving you *honest* feedback.

- Empathetic—I comfort my friend when she's feeling bad
- Encouraging—I remind others of their good qualities
- Funny—I can laugh and be silly
- Generous—I'm quick to share my things and my time
- Honest—I tell the truth, even when it hurts
- Loyal—I stick up for my friends when others make fun of them
- Patient—I don't give up on my friends, even if they're in a bad mood
- Kind—I speak well of others to my friends
- Helpful—I offer to help when I see a friend in need
- Optimistic—I see the good in things; I don't complain or whine a lot
- Compromising—I don't always expect my way but am willing to take turns in choosing things
- Good communicator—I will patiently talk things out when I'm upset instead of just holding a grudge or being argumentative

- Good listener—I hear what people are saying without interrupting
- Fun—I enjoy life and make others happy just being around me
- Wise—I make good decisions and give good advice on the decisions friends are making
- Trustworthy—I keep a secret when I hear one from a friend
- Supportive—I'm excited for my friends when they're interested in an activity

When I look at that list, that's the kind of friend I want to be. But I know I don't always act that way. I can be selfish. Sometimes I say things without thinking. A true friend makes us better.

That's what I want to do for my friends. I want to make them better, sharper. That's what the Bible tells us to do in Proverbs 27:17. We need to act like iron and sharpen each other. And not just our best friends.

Like most of us, Jesus had different levels of friendships. He didn't give all twelve of His disciples bracelets that were etched with the letters *BFF*. He was closest to John and Peter. But He also had His regular group that included the other disciples, as well as Mary, Martha, and Lazarus. Beyond those He had His friendly acquaintances—the crowds of people who came to hear Him speak, watched Him perform miracles, and invited Him to dinner.

List your closest friends . . . the people you'd call if you needed to cry, the friends you can be truly honest with. Most people have only one or two friends who fall into this category. They know everything about you, and you know everything about them.

_____

_____

_____

_____

Now think about the circle beyond that. These are the friends you'd invite to your birthday party. The ones you might sit with at lunch or joke around with in class. You like them and hang out with them pretty often, but you wouldn't share your deepest secrets with them.

_____

_____

_____

_____

Finally, think about the circle beyond that: your friendly acquaintances. These are the people that if you saw them at the store, you'd stop and say hi. You might not know them well enough to invite them to your birthday party, but they'd still go out of their way to say happy birthday to you at school. You're friendly with each other, but you don't hang out much. They might be in your algebra class, on your sports team, or in your church group.

_____

_____

_____

If the people you hang out with most have great friendship qualities, then do a spontaneous cheer and go back to enjoying your friendships.

But after looking at your list, you might fall into one of the following friendship dilemmas.

Dilemma 1: Feeling Friendless

Life can get pretty lonely without good friends. Sometimes we may lose a best friend after a move or when we have to go to a different school or church. Tamika knows exactly what that's like.

Tamika's Story

I'm normally pretty outgoing, but when I first moved to Odyssey, I was supershy. I didn't have any friends. When I got around other girls—even girls who were nice to me—I'd clam up and not know what to say. Or I'd be so nervous, make a really dumb joke, and think, *Why in the world did I say that*? I missed my friends at my other school, so I ended up just trying to be invisible. I didn't talk to anyone, participate in any groups, or even smile much—which is *really* unlike me. Because of that, I didn't get invited to hang out with anyone either, which bummed me out.

We all have times in our lives when we feel friendless. But we don't have to feel that way forever. Here are some of the things we've learned about finding fantastic friends:

OLIVIA: It's okay to be nervous, but just know that other girls are too. Sometimes we think other girls don't like us because they don't say much, when really they're concerned about what we think of them as much as we're worried about what they think of us.

EMILY: Smile and be friendly, even if it feels a little awkward at first. Start conversations with girls you sit next to in class or on the bus. Keep an eye out for girls who might be alone. They're probably looking for friends.

PENNY: Ask questions of others. The best way to learn about somebody is to ask questions. Once she starts talking, you can see what you have in common and take the conversation deeper. If you're not sure how to start a conversation, try a compliment—a genuine one, not empty flattery. Tell her you like her necklace, sweater, gigantic pet poodle, solo at the concert, or whatever.

CAMILLA: I learned the hard way what *doesn't* work. Don't brag about what you have or what you can do. You might think you sound impressive, but really, you're just being obnoxious.

If you want to make new friends, join clubs, sport teams, or groups that interest you. Then when you meet people, you'll already have something in common. Plus, you'll create a strong bond working alongside other people—whether that's putting out a yearbook, winning a volleyball game, or making the perfect scenery for the school play. Remember those interests and talents you listed in chapter 1? Go back to those and think about ways you can bring them out in an organized activity.

When Tamika felt friendless, her mom reminded her to pray for good friends. At first Tamika thought it was kind of silly, but she started praying every morning anyway. Then she started looking around for God's answer, and it seemed like He put the right people at the right time in the right place for her to meet them!

Here's a Secret...

Watch people's body language when you're talking to them. Sometimes that can tell you more than their words do! If someone is looking around, it shows she's bored—or she needs to go to the bathroom and is trying to figure out how to make an exit! If her arms are folded across her chest, it might mean that she's feeling defensive and closed off. If she keeps backing up, it means that you're in her personal space. Everybody has a different comfort level for how close they want people to be to them, so respect that and don't take it personally.

If someone is hunched over or has her shoulders up to her ears, she's probably feeling self-conscious and unsure of herself. Give her a little more time to warm up. And if she's smiling and looking at you—even if she's not saying much—it likely means she's interested in getting to know you better.

Not everyone will want to be your friend. It's okay. That doesn't mean you don't have worth; it simply shows that you're not a good match for everyone. Some personalities click; others not so much. Don't beat yourself up if your potential-friend pick is less than interested. Move on to find the true friends out there who will appreciate you. Don't give up!

And remember, if someone is outright mean to you—rude, mocking, or cruel—that's a problem with who *she* is, not who you are. That's an issue with *her* heart, not a reflection of *your* value. You're worth more, so don't settle for that kind of friend. She's not worth it. Just follow the advice Jesus gave His disciples when a person rejected them: "Shake the dust off your feet" and move on (Matthew 10:14).

Dilemma 2: Friendship Failures

Even if you've been friends with a group of girls for a while, you might get to a point where you realize, *Hey, they're not a very good influence on me.* And you know you need to make a change. Penny had to do just that:

Penny's Story

I moved to Odyssey to attend Campbell College. I didn't have any friends, but I soon met one girl who was pretty nice. She introduced me to a bunch of other art students, and we all started spending a lot of time together. One of my art professors, Dr. Trask, had a discussion group he invited us all to be a part of. I thought I was surrounded with good friends. But then I learned they weren't as great as I thought. In fact, they ended up being involved in a lot of illegal activity. Clearly I needed some new friends—ones I didn't have to testify against in court.*

You'll probably never find a perfect friend, but if you find that your friend often mistreats you, makes fun of you, talks behind your back, or expects you to do things you feel are wrong, you need to be on the lookout for some new friends.

---
* To find out the details, listen to album 53, *The Green Ring Conspiracy*, episodes 679–690.

This can feel pretty overwhelming. After all, you've already found a group of friends you're comfortable with. Change is hard. Starting over in a friendship takes a lot of time, effort, and energy. But if you made one group of friends, you already know you have the ability to click with another group of girls. So make the tough decision to get away from hurtful friends.

Start by looking over the list of important friend qualities from earlier in this chapter. Then take a look at all the people in the different levels of friendship you listed. You might see if you can move some people around. Are there some good friends you could get to know better and possibly become best friends with? Or are there some friendly acquaintances you really respect and say, "Hmm . . . they'd probably make really good friends"? Look for opportunities to get to know these people better. You might not have to abandon your current close friends completely, but you could consider moving them to a different category where they won't have as much influence on you.

As you go through life, your friends will influence your thoughts and actions, so choosing good ones is pretty important. King Solomon, who was far wiser than me, wrote, "He who walks with the wise grows wise, but a companion of fools suffers harm" (Proverbs 13:20).

But even when you have good friends, it doesn't mean there won't be some problems along the way. We'll talk about that next!

Chapter 3

The Joys of Friendship

(Gossiping, Drama Queens, and Frenemies)

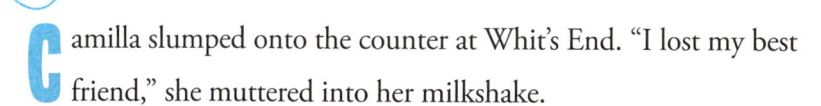

Camilla slumped onto the counter at Whit's End. "I lost my best friend," she muttered into her milkshake.

Before I could console her, Harlow Doyle emerged from under the counter. "Sounds like a case! I'll take it! I'm a private eye, y'know."

"Harlow!" Camilla squealed in surprise. "What were you doing under the counter?"

"Oh, sorry. I was looking for my missing sundae." Harlow gave one last look around. "I was eating it a minute ago, but now all that's left"—he lowered his voice—"is an empty bowl. *Verrrrry peculiar.*"

He hopped onto the stool next to Camilla.

"So where did you last see your friend?"

"In the cafeteria today. Hannah and I always have lunch together."

Harlow began making notes in his detective notebook. "Hmm. So did you misplace her, or do you suspect that she was kidnapped?"

"Neither. She left with some of her other friends."

Harlow scribbled more notes. "Clearly a kidnapping. Who did she leave with?"

"Lisa and Lauren."

"Aha! Our first two suspects. Can you tell me anything about them?"

"They came over to Hannah and started whispering and giggling and looking over at me. Then Hannah said she needed to go, and they left."

"I'm on the case! We'll find your friend or my name isn't Harlow Doyle, pri—"

"Uh, Detective Doyle, my friend wasn't kidnapped," Camilla said sadly. "I'm missing a friend because, well, I don't know if she's my friend anymore."

"Ahh-HA!" Harlow shouted. "From the sound of it, you're

dealing with a frenemy—the friend who turns enemy. How mysterious."

At that point I walked over and started talking to Camilla. The only true mystery she was dealing with was deciphering whether (a) the problem with her friend was something that could be worked through, or (b) she was truly dealing with a frenemy. Frenemies don't really care about your feelings. They're only out to get what's best for them. And those are the kind of "friends" you should let go of.

But how's a girl supposed to know?

Forever Fighting . . .

> OLIVIA: I have a friend who's great most of the time, but we get into fights on a regular basis—usually about something pretty minor. Then we say mean things to each other and end up not talking for a couple of days. Eventually we realize how silly it all is, and we come back together and things are normal again—until our next fight. I'm kinda tired of the drama, though. Should we stop being friends because we fight so much?

Not necessarily. It sounds like for the most part you have a good friend, but you might want to work on communication. Let her know that you want to stop fighting, and talk about ways you can discuss your disagreements instead of losing your tempers.

(Remember your part in this too—after all, it takes two to argue.) You might need to take some cool-down time when you start feeling frustrated, instead of spouting off words you'll regret later. Learn to calmly express how you feel. Like instead of saying, "You never called me back, and I really needed you! You're so selfish!" you could say, "I really hoped to talk to you last night, and I felt hurt that you didn't call back right away."

Even the best of friends sometimes fight. Last Tuesday I needed a break from Penny. I know, I know . . . she's my best friend and roommate, and I absolutely adore her. But I'd just discovered nine Tupperware dishes that held unidentifiable leftovers in the fridge. When I opened one of the containers, it looked like it was growing a miniature rain forest. I even thought I heard a howler monkey. She'd told me a dozen times that she was going to clean out those containers. But everything was still there . . . growing fuzz. So frustrating!

Remember, a perfect friendship is as common as a camel that juggles kittens. Penny and I can annoy each other. Whit and Tom have had arguments. Eugene nearly flipped his lid yesterday when Wooton broke his robot vacuum cleaner. (*Side note:* never try to vacuum out a blender when it's still plugged in.) We all appreciate and love each other—but we still have our problems.

I didn't grow up with sisters or brothers, so I didn't realize how easy it is to disagree, or get into all-out fights, with people you love. Now I understand that's all a part of close relationships. It doesn't mean the friendship is over; it's just a part of having friends. If we deep-down care about each other, most any problem can get worked out.

Even Jesus' group of friends argued.

"I get to sit next to Jesus!"

"Why do I have to pick up all the leftover bread?"

"Hey . . . those are *my* sandals!"

(Well, I might be guessing on some of those, but I don't think people can spend a lot of time together and not have some friendship friction.)

Arguing isn't necessarily a bad thing. It can lead us to better understand each other and help us grow into even better friends. Now that Penny knows what really irritates me (green, mossy leftovers in the fridge, for one), and I know what hurts her feelings (mentioning that her new pants look like clown pants, and the clown was color-blind), we can try to avoid those behaviors. The truth is, you'll have disagreements with people for the rest of your life, so it's best to learn now how to talk through problems and gain a better understanding.

Friends with Friction

But sometimes all the talking in the world won't change the way a person acts. Some kinds of friends are often best to avoid. Read through these four kinds of friends—the Gossip Girl, the Bossing Bestie, the Flip-Around Friend, and the Drama Queen. Do you have any friends who fit these descriptions? Or maybe you'll recognize yourself as you read through how these kinds of friends act. That's okay. When I first became a Christian, I remember somebody at church telling me, "Jesus loves you just the way you are, but He cares about you too much to leave you that way."

God wants us to become more like Him every day. So if you recognize some negative traits in how you act with friends, that can be a good thing. Those are just areas you can work on to become more like Christ.

The Gossip Girl . . .

You'll recognize a Gossip Girl because she often starts conversations with "Did you hear about . . . ?" She's the ruler of rumors and always seems to know a little more than anyone else. Maybe you've even been the victim of a gossip girl. She might act all sympathetic about your bad day, so you spill everything to her about how you fell flat on your face when you tripped on a backpack as you looked over at a boy you like.

Then before you get to your next class, the news is all over school.

I know this girl pretty well because . . . well . . . I was the girl at the lunch table who had the scoop on so-and-so. I loved how everyone looked at me and asked me questions. I'd even make up answers if I didn't know the details. It's like I was addicted to the attention. I wanted others to like me, and I felt like one of the things I could offer was information.

It did get me attention for a while, but it wasn't because people liked me. They just used me to get the dish on other people. Then I realized I was doing the *same* thing. I was using people. Pretty soon my real friends stopped talking to me about their lives. They knew I wasn't trustworthy. And I saw how much I hurt them. I eventually figured out that my reputation and my friendships were more important than being popular. So I gave up on gossip.

Even though it might be fun to get the scoop on others, think about what it's like being the one who's talked about. If your friends start gossiping, or if you get the urge to spread some juicy news you heard, it's good to have other topics for conversation that you can throw out to change the subject. So the next time you hear the lunch-table chatter turn to catty remarks about other people, try some of these conversation changers:

- If you could be really, really good at one thing, what would it be?
- If we were all old enough to go on a trip together anywhere in the world, where would we go?
- If you had one last meal, what would you want to eat?

- What are some of your favorite TV shows or books?
- What's your most embarrassing moment? (That will surely get some laughs.)
- Share a favorite-friend memory. Ask about favorite memories your friends had growing up.
- What animal would you choose if you could have any pet?

You can even say, "I'm trying really hard not to gossip about people, and I'm hoping you can help me." Avoid participating in the rumors. You can't control what other people say, but you can choose to change the subject when someone starts gossiping. You can also choose to get up and leave the conversation. It might feel strange at first, but people will respect you for standing up for your beliefs. They might not admit it right away, but they'll see you're not spreading rumors about others, so they may grow to trust you more with their own secrets.

If you're having trouble figuring out what is and isn't gossip, here are two questions to think about before talking about someone else:

1. Do I know that this information is true?
2. If I were this person, would I want this information spread around?

If you answer no to either question, it's better to leave the story unsaid.

Remember Philippians 4:8, "Whatever is true, whatever is noble, whatever is right, whatever is pure, whatever is lovely, whatever is admirable—if anything is excellent or praiseworthy—think [and talk] about such things."

Here's a Secret...

Sometimes teens start rumors about friends out of jealousy. Like when my friend was selected for the Principal's Award—an honor I'd been hoping for. I found myself saying things like, "I'm not surprised. Her dad is on the school board." And "She's such a teacher's pet. All the teachers think she likes them, but she really doesn't." I went as far as saying, "I can't believe she won even though she almost failed biology first semester."

And this was my friend!

Jealousy makes us do things we never thought we would. (If you don't believe me, take a look at David's story in 2 Samuel 11.) If you feel your friend is spreading gossip about you out of jealousy, talk to her about it. Don't accuse her of being jealous—that never goes well—but ask about how she's feeling and remind her of all the ways you appreciate her as a friend.

The Bossing Bestie . . .

She's the friend who wants things her way . . . or no way. She rolls her eyes at your ideas and assumes you like hers without even asking. If you question her ideas, she makes you feel silly for not going along with her from the start.

Sometimes we're drawn to these seemingly natural-born leaders. Other girls follow them too. They're strong and know what they want. They'll stand up to anyone. The problem comes when they try to tell us what to do all the time or try to pressure us into doing things we don't want to.

Bossy girls like finding friends who are pushovers. Being a pushover isn't the same as being *nice* or being a *peacemaker*. It means we're too afraid or too insecure to express our opinions. And if that's the case, that's not a true friendship.

Here's my number-one tip on dealing with a Bossing Bestie: Be assertive. Instead of saying, "I don't care" or, "Whatever you want," let your opinion be known. Stand up for yourself. Be strong. If she's doing something that hurts your feelings, tell her. If you say something and your friend drops you like a hot ham-and-cheese sandwich, she was never really your friend. She just wanted a sidekick. Sidekicks are good for superheroes, but they don't work in a friendship.

Some Bossing Besties don't realize what they're doing. When you share your opinions and express your feelings, they may recognize their mistakes and realize how valuable your friendship is. That's a friend you can grow with.

Speaking of growing, what if you're the one with the bossing problem? Look at the chart below. Are you a column A person, or do you find yourself living more in column B? If you notice yourself saying a lot of things in column A, you may want to try switching them up with a column B response.

COLUMN A	COLUMN B
I want to do . . .	What do you want to do?
I think that's dumb.	What do you think?
I know how to do this.	How do you think we should do it?

Some friends often argue about little decisions (like what movie you should watch or what snack to make). If that's you, consider having a predetermined way of resolving your disagreements. Play Rock, Paper, Scissors; toss a coin; or leg wrestle. Okay, maybe not that one . .

The Flip-Around Friend . . .

People and relationships go through stages. You're at a time when you're growing a lot—in maturity, personality, even interests. A fortunate few people have the same best friend from first grade through high school graduation, but nearly everyone goes through different stages of life with different friends. It doesn't mean you're less likable. It means people change, and friendships sometimes need to change with you. As hard as it might be to pick yourself up and find a new fabulous friend, the effort is worth it.

But some girls keep going back to a flip-around friend. If that's you, take this *warning*! When a flip-around friend keeps dropping you like a hot panino for another friend but then comes back around, you've got yourself a frenemy. One day she'll be your bestie and want to hang out and share secrets. Then she'll ignore you around other friends. Maybe she'll call you later to apologize, but once you forgive her, she'll make fun of you in front of a crowd of classmates the next day at school. If this sounds like one of your so-called friends, you're better off dropping *her* like a hot slice of cheese pizza. This girl is using you for what she wants or needs at the time, but she has no interest in being a true friend. Trust me. You can do better.

Let's hear a story from Tamika:

Tamika's Story

In fifth grade, my best friend was Makayla. We had so much fun together! We made up cupcake recipes and were always getting into trouble about the messes we made. We had sleepovers, took swimming lessons together, and laughed a *lot*. At the beginning of sixth grade, Megan moved to our school. Makayla and I ended up becoming friends with her, too. Then it was the three of us hanging out at each other's houses and baking cupcakes. But I started noticing something that spring: Makayla and Megan passing notes to each other in class or whispering to each other at lunch. I'd ask what they were talking about. Sometimes they'd tell me, but other times they'd shrug and say, "Oh, nothing." Soon they started going to movies together and having overnights without inviting me. It didn't take long before I realized they were M&M's that no longer included me.

The Drama Queen . . .

We all know this girl. She's constantly in the middle of some huge, dramatic situation. A boy likes her so much, it's driving her to the brink of insanity. A former friend is out to get her. A teacher assigns more homework than any teacher *ever*. A choir director refuses to give her a solo. She'll be devastated by someone's dirty look or furious about a rumor that she's sure is being passed around about her. And if you question the validity of her concerns, she'll burst into tears and call you "the worst friend ever." Oh, and this all takes place before first period! Although the drama queen has no trouble keeping a conversation going, you find yourself wondering, *How much of this is for real?*

Probably not much. These are the friends who get upset with you over small things and exaggerate the flaws in others. They constantly feel ignored, betrayed, and overwhelmed. They might be entertaining . . . but they're *exhausting*.

Emotions run high as we get into adolescence, so we all feel oversensitive at times. Occasional fits of the dramatic can be normal. But when it feels like this is something you're dealing with multiple times a week, you likely have a friend who's a class A Drama Queen.

Have a chat with the Drama Queen. Let her know you care about her as a friend and want to hear her problems. Be honest by telling her that sometimes your relationship can be draining.

Instead of seeing the worst in everything, encourage her to trust God and work through her problems. If she's having a dramatic meltdown, remove yourself from the situation, but let her know that you're praying for her. If she gets angry with you for your comments or continues to blow up, change the subject, get off the phone, or simply excuse yourself. When her theatrics aren't rewarded with the attention she's after, she might think twice before putting on a show.

What It All Comes Down To . . .

Think back to those questions you answered in chapter 1. Do your friends line up with who you are and who you want to be? Do they encourage you to grow in positive ways, or do they pressure you to go against your beliefs? Do you feel like you're growing more into your "three qualities" (page 13) when you're with them, or do you find yourself trying to fit into a mold they want to put you in? Answer these questions honestly and decide if your friendships are ones worth investing in for the long haul.

Chapter 4

Get the Garlic out of Your Pudding

(Learning to Lead)

You may have noticed that most of Penny's and my disagreements start in the refrigerator. Not with *us* in the refrigerator—that would be a little cramped—but with things we put into the refrigerator.

For instance, I made a lovely vanilla pudding the other day. I mixed it up in the morning and placed it on the middle shelf to eat after dinner. Penny later made some of her famous pasta sauce—which includes a *lot* of garlic. She minced up a bit too much garlic and didn't want to waste it. So as her sauce simmered, she placed the rest of the raw garlic in the fridge.

On the top shelf. Then she accidentally bumped the plate and caused some of the garlic to fall onto the second shelf.

More specifically, it fell into my pudding.

Guess what my face looked like when I took a huge bite of my long-awaited pudding that night? Whatever you're imagining, I looked ten times worse. My throat closed up. My eyes bulged out. Tears streamed down my cheeks. And I think my hair may have even stood on end.

Seriously, it was like tasting garlic pudding. The vanilla flavor had disappeared. Instead of savoring my delicious vanilla pudding, I ended up with a mouthful of sweet and slimy garlic sauce.

Garlic has a tendency to take over. If you've ever cooked with it or eaten it, you know a little goes a long way, and the flavor tends to stick around.

Our friends can have a similar effect. Not only do they tend to stick around, but we often take on the *flavor* of those we hang out with. Without even realizing it, we may start acting like them. If you have a friend who always tosses her hair and says, "Skippity, dippity," don't be surprised if you start saying and doing the same thing. We often take on the characteristics of the people closest to us. That's why the apostle Paul warned us in the Bible, "Bad company corrupts good character" (1 Corinthians 15:33). If we have friends who are negative and sarcastic, we many end up more that way too.

The opposite is also true. Friends who are thoughtful and cheery often draw out those characteristics inside us. Penny's been a good friend in that way. She's full of joy, acts selflessly, and is kindhearted. Being around her makes me want to act more like Jesus. She's the kind of friend we should all want to hang around—people who encourage our relationship with Christ.

But I've had friends who have pulled me in the other direction. These friends used bad language, listened to music with gross lyrics, consistently gossiped, and criticized others. Without even realizing it, I started doing the same things.

Listen to what Olivia did when this happened to her.

Olivia's Story

In seventh grade, I started hanging out with some girls in my algebra class—Gina and McKenna. They showed me how to do my hair in fun ways and introduced me to mascara.

Every day before school, they'd drag me into the bathroom, pull out a bunch of makeup from their backpacks, and spend ten minutes putting stuff all over our faces. It was kinda fun. Then I started noticing a few things. Our conversations always seemed to include stuff we saw in fashion magazines and what outfits we were going to wear the next day.

The more I hung out with Gina and McKenna, the more I became concerned with how I looked. I began spending more money on clothes and accessories. I had to reapply my lip gloss after every class. I'd take an hour every morning styling (and restyling) my hair. I know it's okay to care about how you look, but I pretty much became obsessed. I began skipping my time with God in the morning and stopped going to sign-language club before school so I could spend more time in front of the mirror. Then I quit the swim team because I didn't want to get my hair wet. One afternoon I finally woke up and thought, *Wait, what am I doing? I love swimming more than perfectly styled hair.* I made some lasting changes. I still like Gina and McKenna, but I don't hang out with them as much as I used to. I just didn't want my outlook on life to be centered on looks.

Olivia's smart for recognizing how important it is to choose friends who have values we admire—because it's very likely that over time, we're going to wind up acting more like them.

Your Turn

How easily influenced are you? Take the following quiz to find out.

1. You really like wearing your hair in a braid, but one day a popular girl at school remarks that your hairstyle is babyish. The next day you . . .
    A. wear it the same way. Who cares what anyone else thinks? It's your hair!
    B. wear it down and straight. You might try the braid again sometime, but not until you figure out a more grown-up way of doing it.
    C. style it just like that popular girl at school, because she obviously knows what's in.

2. You just met a girl in your English class who seems really nice. You want to invite her to hang out with you and your friends. When you bring it up with them, they talk about how nerdy the girl dresses and how someone once saw her picking her nose, so you . . .

A. defend the girl. Just because she dresses differently doesn't mean she won't be fun to hang out with.
B. laugh it off, saying, "Yeah, I guess we wouldn't want to be seen with someone like that!" After all, there's no point in upsetting your friends.
C. change the subject. Maybe you'll ask the girl to come over sometime when your other friends aren't around.

3. A group of people in your grade meet to discuss the design for your class float. Someone suggests a zoo theme, and a lot of kids get excited about it. You had some other ideas. With everyone watching, your friend turns and asks what you think. You . . .
    A. smile and agree with everyone else. "A zoo theme would be perfect." No sense even mentioning your ideas.
    B. shrug and say, "I was thinking about a winter wonderland theme, but now that seems kinda dumb. Let's go with the zoo idea."
    C. enthusiastically say, "A zoo could be fun, but what about a winter wonderland theme? We could have an igloo and snowmen and even use a snow machine to blow out snow." Even if your idea gets turned down, you want to express yourself.

4. A trend around school has everyone wearing orange, plastic bracelets. You think they look pretty tacky, so you . . .
    A. use up two weeks' worth of allowance to buy some. You don't want to be the only one not wearing them.
    B. shop for some bracelets you really like. Why waste money on something you don't even want?
    C. buy a bright necklace. Maybe you can start your own fashion trend.

5. A popular girl invited you to her very exclusive party! The only problem is, her parents won't be home, and you know *your* parents won't approve. "Don't worry about it," she tells you. "Everyone else is telling their parents that my mom is chaperoning. You want to come, don't you?" You say:
    A. "I really want to come. Hopefully my parents won't ask about your parents. But if they do, I'll have to tell them the truth. So I'm not sure if I'll be there or not."
    B. "Thanks for the invite, but I'm not okay with lying to my parents. I won't be able to come."
    C. "Of course. If my parents ask, I'll just make something up. See you Friday!"

6. A good friend of yours tends to let a curse word slip out pretty often. You . . .

A. find yourself saying the word too. It's not that big of a deal as long as your mom doesn't hear it.
B. catch her when she says it and let your friend know that it bothers you.
C. notice that same word coming to mind when you're mad. You don't say it out loud, but it's hard to control your mouth!

Score It

1. A=3, B=2, C=1   _____
2. A=3, B=1, C=2   _____
3. A=1, B=2, C=3   _____
4. A=1, B=2, C=3   _____
5. A=2, B=3, C=1   _____
6. A=1, B=3, C=2   _____
   Total   _____

Add Up Your Score

Here's how to interpret your score:

6–9: Uh-oh. You're overly influenced by those around you. Even though it might not seem like a big deal right now, it's likely that you'll also be influenced in more dangerous ways in the years to come. Practice standing up for what's right. It will be hard at first, but you might be surprised at how much more your friends will respect you.

10–14: Not quite a standout. You have a good heart and know the right thing to do, but you sometimes cave under pressure. Watch out for speaking half-truths and not standing up for your convictions. You have the potential to be a positive leader, so keep working at it!

15–18: Great job! You know how to speak your mind and be a true leader—influencing people in a positive direction. Continue growing in confidence and being a healthy example to others.

Be a Leader

How did you do on the quiz? Remember that peer pressure isn't always a bad thing. It can influence people to act in harmful ways *or* to make good decisions. Whit's positive influence on me helped me become a Christian. The influence of my mom and grandma encouraged me to make the right decisions. And my friends nudged me to try new things: snorkeling, writing a book, and eating a peanut-butter, cucumber, and licorice sandwich (that last one was Wooton, in case you didn't guess).

The important thing is choosing your friends and influencers wisely. Make sure you're hanging around people you want to be like! And don't forget that you can be an influencer yourself. If you spend time only with people who share your convictions, it can be difficult to make a difference for God's kingdom. Shine your light in places that need hope. But remember not to leave your faith behind. Christ gives you the power to be a leader.

Just to clarify . . . I don't mean a leader who is domineering, bossy, self-righteous, and insists on things being done her way. In fact, that's not really being a leader at all. That's being a pain.

A leader isn't . . .

- the loudest person
- the one who knows it all
- someone who talks more than everyone else
- someone who never makes a mistake
- arrogant

A leader is . . .

- someone who speaks up and shares her beliefs
- someone who consistently encourages others to speak their thoughts
- someone who seeks input from others
- someone who stands up against wrongdoing
- someone who leads by example
- a person who serves others and builds them up

First Timothy 4:12 explains that leadership isn't only for older people or government officials. According to the apostle Paul, you can be a leader right now. Here's what he said: "Don't let anyone look down on you because you are young, but set an example for the believers in speech, in life, in love, in faith and in purity."

Even if you're young, you can be an influencer by showing people how to live the abundant lives Christ has planned for us. Tamika has a great story on how she was a leader in an unexpected way.

Tamika's Story

I never thought of myself as a leader. I'm pretty shy in groups. But the other day a boy in my class tripped this girl who was a couple of years younger—then laughed at her. It made me furious. I walked over and said, "Why do you need to pick on people? That was so rude—and not at all funny!" He just smirked at me. I looked around, realizing everyone in the crowded hallway heard me. They were all staring. At first I kinda wanted to shut myself up in a locker. Then a funny thing happened: They started agreeing with me. "Yeah, grow up," a boy said. "Tamika's right," another girl added. I learned that being a leader isn't really about how much you say but when you say it. People respect someone who stands up for what's right. And I earned a lot of respect that day.

Here's a Secret...

Leadership isn't about a position. You don't need to be the president, a movie star, or a genius to have influence. Leadership is really about the person you prove yourself to be through your words and actions. Are you someone worth imitating?

Being a leader might not be easy. For some of you, just thinking about it makes your palms sweat a bit. You're not alone. One of the greatest leaders of all time didn't want the job. Remember Moses? He led millions of Israelites for over forty years! But when God called him to be a leader, he said, "Who am I?"

Moses didn't believe he was qualified to lead God's people. He didn't have the confidence to stand up to Pharaoh. He begged God to choose someone else because he didn't think he was a gifted speaker or a powerful enough person.

"O Lord, please send someone else to do it," Moses said (Exodus 4:13).

But God knew He had the right man for the job. More than an articulate leader, God wanted someone who would be obedient. God didn't need a powerful person, just a person who would rely on the power that comes from following Him.

Eventually, with a little convincing, Moses was willing to step up and be a leader. He sought God's will as he made decisions and guided the Israelites. Over and over again, he acted in obedience. That's what made him a great leader.

Just as God helped Moses become a great leader, He can bring out the leader in you, too.

Chapter 5

Crying into My Pizza

(Understanding Cliques)

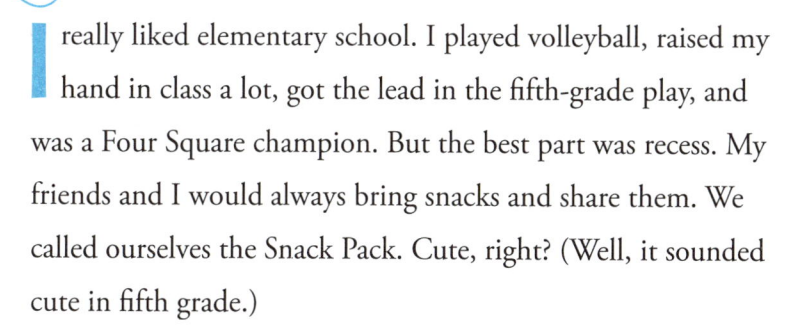

I really liked elementary school. I played volleyball, raised my hand in class a lot, got the lead in the fifth-grade play, and was a Four Square champion. But the best part was recess. My friends and I would always bring snacks and share them. We called ourselves the Snack Pack. Cute, right? (Well, it sounded cute in fifth grade.)

The summer before I started sixth grade, my family moved

to a different neighborhood—away from my friends. I missed seeing them all summer, so I was extraexcited about going back to school. I just knew everything would go back to how it had always been: having lunch with my friends, passing notes in class, going to slumber parties on weekends.

That first day, I headed over to my group of friends with my tray of pizza and applesauce.

"Hey, Snack Pack!" I said.

My friends stopped gabbing, looked up at me, and then broke out in giggles. But not "So great to see you" giggles. These were "We're laughing *at* you" giggles. That's when I noticed they were all wearing the same silver, dangly earrings; bright-pink T-shirts; and overdone eyeliner.

One of my friends moved her purse into the one empty seat to block me from sitting down. Then everyone went back to talking, never even giving me a second glance. Clearly I was no longer welcome.

Tears pricked my eyes, but I knew I couldn't cry in front of them. I turned and looked for another table. But I soon realized there was no other table for me. Everyone else had their group, their friends. Except me. Worse, a lump was growing in my throat. I was terrified I'd burst into tears any second. Somehow I managed to keep everything together until I left the cafeteria, passed the gym, and ducked into the girls' locker room. I crouched down on the bench at the end of the room and let the tears spill into my pepperoni pizza.

For the next few weeks, that's where I ate lunch. Every day. I never told my parents because I didn't want to burden them. (I know now what a bad choice that was, because my mom would've been a great help.)

After downing my lunch in silence, I'd *slowly* go back to my locker. Then I'd *slowly* walk into the office to see if Mrs. Pritchett, the school secretary, needed me to run errands for her. After that, I'd *slowly* shuffle to the bathroom—*anything* to fill in lunchtime without being noticed.

I eventually got over it and found some new friends to hang out with. But it still hurts to think about how my Snack Pack friends discarded me like an empty Snickers wrapper.

Clicking with a Clique

Have you ever met somebody and just clicked? I have. Penny and I were sort of that way. When a group of clicky people band together, it's called a *clique*. Eugene told me the expression came from an old French word that means "a sharp noise." Penny thought that noise might have been a high-pitched squeal of "Ohhh! Let's hang out together."

Cliques aren't necessarily bad. We all want to belong to something bigger than ourselves. God designed us to desire relationship and live in community with others. You could even say that Jesus and His disciples were a clique.

Cliques often form around a mutual interest or value—like computers, drama, athletics, or band. Cliques can be good. They can encourage us to develop our talents and support us through difficult times. It's comfortable to have our spot where we're known, liked, and accepted. We can walk into the gym or cafeteria knowing our friends will make room for us and be happy to see us. Plus, it's great to know that we have a set of friends to make plans with.

But there's a downside to cliques too. The girls in cliques can be mean to outsiders. When cliques become exclusive—and rude about it—it's a problem. Clicky people may act superior to other kids and reject those who want to be a part of their group. Other times, a clique can turn against its own members. One day you're accepted by the group, laughing and having a great time. The next day, members of the clique turn their backs on you and don't let you sit at their table, like the Snack Pack that turned against me. Some cliques can push us to do things that go against our values. All it takes is the leader of the group to decide that something is cool—like seeing a certain movie, drinking, or smoking—and suddenly everybody else wants to try it.

And often there's one clique that seems like "the place to be," but even that can be disappointing. Just ask Olivia.

Olivia's Story

I was always kind of envious of the cool crowd. It seemed like there was something magical about being *popular*. I thought if I could only be in that group, all of my problems would disappear. Then the unexpected happened: I ended up becoming friends with a couple of popular girls through a play I was in. They even invited me to sit with their group during lunch! When I sat at their table, I no longer felt invisible. It felt like everyone was looking at me. I was ecstatic! For about a week. Because that's how long it took to realize that being in the popular crowd didn't end my problems; it created new ones. A lot of the popular girls wanted to talk, but not one of them really listened to me—unless I was telling them how I thought their speech was so amazing, or their clothes were so perfect, or their haircut was so beautiful. Conversations were never that interesting. They'd either be about how great they were or how dorky everyone else was. Instead of feeling like

I had a lot of friends, I started feeling really lonely. And I realized that a lot of the popular girls were lonely too. They just disguised it well.

Eventually I ended up back at my old table with my old friends. As nice as it was to have people think I was popular, it was way better to actually be myself, have fun, and hang out with friends who really cared about me.

Here's a Secret...

No one goes through adolescence without insecurity. No one. We disguise it in different ways. Being mean to others. Acting arrogant. Becoming part of the cool crowd and trying to make others feel inferior. Putting on an aloof and bored front. Hiding behind lots of makeup or fashionable clothes.

Don't think you're the only one who feels self-conscious. Everyone wishes they could change something about their looks or their lives. Try to live according to an old prayer: accept the things you can't change, change the things you can, and have the wisdom to know the difference between the two.

Making Cliques Work for You, Not Against You

You've probably noticed the *cool* groups at your school or even at your church. Most everyone knows who these kids are and wants to be their friends. Everyone knows the cool kids have the power to influence others. One thing to remember about the popular group is that they only have "power" because others give it to them. They're truly *not* better than anyone else—and they're definitely not better in God's eyes. He loves and values us equally.

As you decide what group you best fit into, remember who you are in Christ. You're His masterpiece. You're a princess of the King of Kings. Look for where you can honor God, grow closer to Him, and develop into the young lady He created you to be. With that in mind . . .

Choose the right group. Although it's tempting to fall into the group where you're already known or the first place you're accepted, it's best to find the group that lines up with who you want to be. Early on, it's important to look for kids you really enjoy and can be yourself around. Because as you get into high school, it can become more uncomfortable to switch cliques.

Don't change your beliefs. Cliques often resort to *groupthink*. That means everyone starts forming the same opinions—like when my Snack Pack started dressing alike, wearing makeup, and ignoring me. Whatever group you're in, don't lose who you are. Remember those gifts and dreams and beliefs you wrote about in chapter 1. You were created with different talents, abilities, and skills from everyone else. You're not poured into the same mold like a Jell-O cup. You've been given unique interests, thoughts, and opinions. Be proud of how God designed you!

Start out by making friends with people, not groups. After I came out of the girls' locker room, I started talking to this girl who sat next to me in science class. We had a great time being lab partners. Then she introduced me to her group of friends, who were really nice and lots of fun. Approaching a whole lunch table full of girls can be scary, so it's a lot easier to befriend just one person.

Your Turn

Take some time today to pray for your friends. Pray that they will remain faithful to follow God throughout their teen years and beyond. Ask God to bring the right girls into your life, girls who will be a good influence on you. Write out your prayer below.

_____

_____

_____

_____

Now think of some people you know who get picked on at school by the kids in cliques. Write down their names and pray for them. Jot down some ideas on how you can be an encouragement to them.

_____

_____

_____

_____

_____

_____

Turning My Back on the Pack

A couple of years after the Snack Pack removed me from their "lunch box," my mom and I ended up moving to Odyssey. I had to start all over finding a new group of girls. This time I ended up with the best friends of my life. And it's where I learned the most important lesson about cliques.

During my sophomore year, I met Ashley. She was on the yearbook staff and usually ate her lunch with other writer types. I started sitting with them and quickly realized how much I enjoyed their company. One Friday night, Ashley invited me to join her and a couple of her friends at the school's football game. We burrowed under blankets, ate hot dogs, and cheered for our team. That's all pretty normal, but one thing stood out about Ashley. She greeted practically everyone who walked by. Her conversation wasn't limited to the group of friends around her. She talked to Cooper—the kid who practically lived in the computer lab—in the same friendly way she chatted with Sydney, the head cheerleader.

After halftime, we maneuvered our way to the concession stand for some popcorn. Ashley said hi to the girls running the Pep Club table, congratulated a few band members on a great halftime show, and went out of her way to meet a few kids who were sitting apart from the crowd. She didn't know everyone's name, but that didn't stop her from being friendly.

Ashley was simply being herself. She hadn't gotten sucked into groupthink, blindly following the same opinions, ideas, and likes or dislikes as everyone in her group. She maintained who she was as a person. If her clique ever turned on her (like mine did), she had other friends. But more important, she wasn't controlled by her clique. She kept her own personality and values. And here's the amazing thing: people respected her for it. While other students were concerned about who was in or out, Ashley just enjoyed people. Because of that, a lot of people liked her.

I knew that's what I wanted too. Ashley ended up being a great friend. We'd eat lunch together, attend church events, and always make a point of going to football games. She even visited me when I started working at Whit's End. But I also enjoyed seeing other friends—from the computer club to the marching band to the baseball jocks.

Sometimes as part of a clique, we're encouraged to ignore other groups that are labeled nerds or losers. But when you treat others rudely, you cut off the possibilities of more friendships. Not to mention that it makes you kind of a loser yourself.

Never Alone

As awesome as Ashley was, Jesus is our ultimate role model—in how to act, speak, pray, be a friend . . . really everything. He had His group—the disciples—but He was never exclusive with them. He sought out all types of people. He'd hang out with Nicodemus (a respected religious leader), Zacchaeus (an unpopular tax collector), and Mary Magdalene (a woman with a questionable past). He'd have dinner with politicians, lepers, the rich, and the poor. He didn't favor those who had more popularity, power, or money. In fact, He could be harsh with leaders who abused their power or took advantage of other people.

Jesus can relate to you no matter where you are on the clique spectrum. At times He was wildly popular, to the point that it exhausted Him. People lined up to have Him over for dinner, talk to them, or heal their illnesses.

Other times, Jesus found Himself alone and abandoned by even His closest friends. One of His own disciples betrayed Him for a little money. Then Peter, one of His best friends, denied knowing Jesus when He needed Peter most. Talk about frenemies! Jesus was also bullied, spit on, mocked, and nearly killed by people from His hometown. Jesus experienced all of the ups and downs of relationships. So wherever you are on the clique spectrum—from feeling friendless to overly popular—remember that you're not alone.

Chapter 6

Adventures of the Nerd Bird

(How to Handle a Mean Girl)

On the picnic day, we got some visitors.

Olivia spotted them first. "Look who's here."

"Katrina!" I shouted, jumping up. "Katreeeeeena!"

Dozens of people looked my way as Katrina Meltsner headed over to the picnic blanket I was sharing with Olivia, Penny, and the rest of the girls. Sure, I saw Eugene, Wooton, and Jason with her. But I was just interested in some girl talk right then.

"I heard you, Connie." Katrina chuckled. "I believe everybody within a three-mile radius heard you."

"Try this egg-salad sandwich I made," Penny said as Katrina walked up.

She took a sandwich from Penny and bit into it.

"Do you notice anything dill-icious about it?" Penny asked.

"I notice something different," Katrina said. She was still smiling, but I could see that she had stopped chewing.

"So do you want to hang out with us and ditch those guys?" I said, joking.

"Honestly, it would be a welcome relief," Katrina said. "We're here searching for the best place to set up the picnic tables Whit's End is donating to the park. It's exhausting."

"Why is that so difficult?" Olivia asked.

"Oh, you know Eugene. He has binders of topographical maps to find the most level spots. Jason wants the shadiest spots. And Wooton is looking to put all the tables closest to the candy store."

"That could take awhile," I acknowledged, imagining the discussion among the three. "I was just telling Olivia about some of the stuff I went through in middle school. What were you like as a teen?"

It didn't take much prodding to get Katrina to spill about her early teen years. I couldn't believe all the things she had to deal with . . . and I wished that the today me could have known her in seventh grade.

Katrina's Story

Most of the time, I felt quite a bit different from my peers in middle school. I enjoyed studying and attending class—and constantly had my nose in a book. That made me an easy target for those who wanted someone to torment. I didn't care so much about the latest fashions or even, though I hate to admit it now, brushing my hair. I also had a face full of pimples. One day during science class, the teacher showed us photos of birds. A picture came up of the marabou stork—an awkward-looking bird with paltry feathers, a massive beak, and a bumpy red face. A girl named Emma in the back of the class shouted out, "That looks like Katrina Shanks!" Everyone laughed. Soon the entire school was calling me Nerd Bird. Emma was typically surrounded by a group of girls. Nearly every week, they came up with a new nickname for me: Latrina, Smelly Shanks, Geeky Glasses. I attended an elite, private school, and my parents mistakenly thought students there would be above acting cruelly, but I think every school probably has a quantifiable amount of verbal bullying.

Initially I tried to ignore the name-calling. But those words began to really sting. I tried to avoid Emma and her group, but they found me anyway. I asked them politely to stop, but it only got worse. They'd throw things at me whenever a teacher turned her back. They'd giggle loudly every time I answered a question in class. I didn't like being the outsider, so I decided to change. And what a change it was! I begged my mother to take me shopping for expensive, trendy clothes. I didn't even like them, but they were what Emma wore. I had my hair cut into this spiky bob that was popular. Ugh . . . it looked awful on me. I globbed makeup all over my pimples, threw out my glasses, and went to the optometrist to get fitted for contacts—even though they made my eyes water. I quit the Math Bowl and quiz team. Eventually I began intentionally missing questions on tests so the teacher wouldn't point me out as having a perfect score.

But Emma and her group *still* made fun of me. Now they called me a *wannabe*, since I was trying to look like them. The names didn't go away. In fact, I was more miserable because now I'd given up the things I truly did enjoy.

Thankfully I had a friend, Joleen, who was a couple of years older than I was. We'd been on the quiz team together. She found me crying behind the school one day and put her arm around me. "Is the point of your life for Emma to be happy with you, or for you to be happy with you?"

Truthfully, at that point, all I wanted to do was survive Emma. Being invisible would have been a welcome relief. But I knew what Joleen was saying. Emma was cruel and mean. Why should I give her the power to impact my life? I certainly wouldn't want to be like her. I didn't need her to like me. I needed me to like me.

And *I* liked me with glasses, my regular jeans, and button-down shirts. So I grew out my regular hairstyle and rejoined the clubs I enjoyed. Joleen helped too, by reminding me there were things I could do to give the obnoxious people less ammunition. By keeping my hair neat and treating my acne, it not only gave people fewer things to make fun of, but it also built my confidence.

I started hanging out with people on the Math Bowl team who appreciated my desire for knowledge and my quirky sense of humor. I even enlisted a couple of team members to walk down the halls with me. When I wasn't alone, I became less of a target for Emma and her crew. (Not unlike antelope who are off on their own and become prey for lions, I suppose.) And even when they did call out a name, I could pretend to be immersed in conversation and not even acknowledge it.

Emma soon tired of picking on me, and except for an occasional muttered "Nerd Bird," she left me alone. Ironically, when I interned at my father's company the summer after graduation, Emma was one of the employees I supervised. Hmm . . . she was much nicer then.

Neither Sticks Nor Stones

Katrina's story reminded me a little of my own. It's never fun being a target. Unfortunately, every school has a mean girl—or several. These are the "pretty bullies." Instead of the tough kid pushing others around on the playground demanding their lunch money, the mean girl uses words, taunts, texts, tweets, and influence to pick on others. So even though you're unlikely to get a bruise from a mean girl, the wounds from her words can hurt far worse and last far longer.

Many times a mean girl is friendly, well liked by teachers, and nice to most people. But she'll select a handful of unfortunate girls to bully. And she often gets her friends to join her.

Sometimes we're not sure whether we're being bullied. So here's the definition. *Bullying* is repeatedly and intentionally hurting another person. This could be done physically—like someone pulling your hair, pushing you, or tripping you. But mean girls often avoid the physical. Their bullying is of the emotional variety: teasing, taunting, starting rumors about you, calling you names, getting others to ignore you. They can hurt you without even saying a word, like when someone continually turns her back on you or gives you the talk-to-the-hand gesture.

Bullying is different from someone simply being rude to you, because bullying is ongoing and on purpose, not just a one-time mean statement or an occasional eye roll.[1]

I've run across my share of mean girls—both when I was in school and even at Whit's End. Some of the things you might hear a mean girl say are . . .

- "You can't sit there. That seat's reserved."
- "Who taught you how to put on makeup . . . a clown?"
- "Have you ever heard of Clearasil, because you should use it."
- "Have you seen her lately?! That hairstyle is so last year!"
- "Do you know how to use deodorant?"
- "I can't believe she's wearing that. I had that outfit . . . when I was six!"
- "My mom's making me invite her, but we're all planning on ditching her once we get there."
- "No one likes being around her. I hope you don't talk to her anymore."
- "She's such a loser."

But... why?

For most mean girls, being cruel makes them feel powerful. They like embarrassing people or seeing if they can make someone cry. And they're usually surrounded by friends who go along with them. Not because the friends agree with the mean girl but because they're terrified that they'll be the next victims. They think they can avoid getting picked on by focusing the attention on somebody else.

The ironic thing is, mean girls are about the most insecure girls you'll ever meet. Picking on others gives them a sense of control over their lives and other people. They need that feeling because they don't really like who they are. Mean girls commonly struggle with feeling unlovable or like they don't measure up. So those hurt feelings come out in hurting other people.

Mean girls may also choose victims they're jealous of—like the girl who just got her braces off and is really pretty, or the one who "stole" the coveted solo in the choir concert. When a mean girl feels threatened, she'll lash out by making up rumors, spreading lies, and picking on the girl in hopes that her self-esteem will plummet.

As much as we hate to admit it, we've all been mean girls to some extent. Maybe you've had an attitude with your mom or said hurtful things to your brother because you had a bad day at school. Maybe you've told one friend negative things about another friend because you're jealous of her. It's a common misconception that hurting other people will make us feel better. The truth? It doesn't. In fact, it makes us feel awful.

God wants us to "encourage one another and build each other up" (1 Thessalonians 5:11). When we build up the people around us, they may like us more. But if we're cruel or think only of ourselves, we may end up miserable and friendless.

Here's a Secret...

Have you ever looked at a girl and thought, *She's got it all. She's rich and pretty and has a lot of friends. There's no way she'd feel insecure.* If you've thought that, think again. No one has a perfect life. Everyone you see in your classroom, every person you pass at the mall, every teacher, every adult, every kid has his or her own hurt and fears. You just don't know what they are. Maybe their parents fight a lot. Maybe they have a parent who recently lost a job. Maybe they feel like nobody knows who they really are, and so they have to keep putting on an act. They might be secretly worried that they're not all that smart or special, and people will find them out.

We've All Been There

After hearing Katrina's story, Olivia said everyone has been the victim of a mean girl at some point. So I went around the picnic blanket asking the girls what they'd learned about handling girl bullies:

> EMILY: The first time I got picked on, I ran away crying. That was *not* the right thing to do. Because then the girl realized how much power she had over me. That's exactly what she wanted, so the teasing only got worse. Every day after school, the mean girl's group would find me and make fun of me. My mom suggested that I practice coming up with responses that would throw off my tormentors. What worked for me was saying things in a bored voice like, "Don't worry, you'll grow out of this bullying stage." Or saying, "I can't believe this is what you do for fun." Sometimes just smiling and shaking my head worked. It didn't take too long for my bully to realize she couldn't upset me anymore. That took all the fun out of it for her, and she gave up picking on me.
>
> PENNY: I was bullied pretty badly by some girls when I moved to a new school. I was artsy and dressed a little quirky, so that made me an easy target. One thing I learned is that mean girls are less likely to pick on you when you're near adults or with friends. My bullies seemed to bug me only

when I was alone. So I tried to hang out where teachers were in earshot and surrounded myself with a few friends when I could. I found other artsy kids who had also been picked on. We'd team up to walk places. When we were together, the bullies left us alone, because there's strength in numbers.

OLIVIA: I knew trying to reason with my bully or tell her how much her actions hurt me wouldn't help. But one thing I did was pray for the mean girl. It was the hardest thing I ever did, because I *really* didn't like her, and her teasing kept getting worse and worse. I'd remind myself that Jesus told us to "bless those who curse you, pray for those who mistreat you" (Luke 6:28). I'd also quote Psalm 28:7 to myself when she'd pick on me. I'd say, "The Lord is my strength and my shield," over and over, remembering that even though I couldn't see Him, God was there. He was on my side, and He cared about me.

Your Turn

God's Word can help you through any difficulty you face. When bullies try to make your life miserable, dig into the Bible to find joy and a peace that surpasses understanding.

Psalm 28:7 would be a great verse to add to your journal, tape up on your bathroom mirror, write on your notebook, and memorize. Here are some other verses that might help:

- Romans 12:19-21
- 2 Timothy 1:7
- Isaiah 41:10

Here are responses from the other girls:

Camilla: I made the mistake of trying to laugh along with the bullies, like I agreed. That's fine, I guess, if your friends are teasing you for fun. But when someone is really being cruel, if you act like you agree, it only gets worse. I thought I was supposed to be nice, but my mom told me that I could also be strong. Jesus often stood up to bullies when they were picking on others. And He feels the same way about you. It's never okay for someone to be cruel to you. After I talked with my mom, the next time the mean girl started her taunts, I turned to her and said, "You may feel the need to pick on someone today, but that someone is not going to be me." And I left. She never bothered me again.

Katrina: Don't believe what a bully says about you. Talking to other girls who've been bullied—and there are a lot of us—I realized that we sometimes start believing the lies. *Maybe no one* does *like me. Maybe I* am *a science nerd.* Don't allow bullies the power to define you. That right belongs only to the God who made you—and He says you are of incredible value. You don't need to sit and listen to someone degrade you. Leave.

TAMIKA: Practice acting confident—even when you don't feel it. Bullies are drawn to kids who look insecure. Practice standing straight, walking purposefully, and looking up and around, not down at your feet. Music also helped me. When bullies got me down, I listened to uplifting songs. I'd sing along and feel empowered and encouraged by the music.

There really isn't one surefire way to ward off a bully. So you might need to try a few different things. But here are some other good reminders whenever you're being picked on:

1. *This is temporary.* Bullying is at its worst from sixth to eighth grade. Girls generally start outgrowing it in high school, and it's way less common in college.[2] Some girls who are tormented by mean girls start believing that life will always be this way. They might contemplate making self-destructive choices. But put these years of your life in perspective. Middle school is only a short blip in your long life. You have many, many great years of friends and memories to come. If you think about it this way, it might help you get through some rough days.

2. *You're not alone.* Nearly every adult you talk to probably went through a time when they were teased. Yet, they all

survived. Some people look back and even believe they grew into stronger, more compassionate human beings because they were bullied.

Bullying goes way back to biblical times. Read through Psalm 55, and you might find David saying a few things you're feeling yourself!

3. *This is not about you.* Bullying is about someone who wants to feel important and is desperately trying to find some self-worth. You're just caught in the crossfire. Don't believe the words that you're ugly, dumb, or a loser. I know the words still hurt. As much as you can, remind yourself about what we talked about in chapter 1. Go back to what you journaled. Remember who you *really* are.

"Sticks and stones may break my bones, but words will never hurt me" is a lie. Words *do* hurt. Even though people might tell you to "just ignore it," that's way easier said than done. It's normal that hurtful words bother you, and it's wrong—*really* wrong—for people to relentlessly pick on you. So a time might come when you need to tell an adult. And that's okay. In fact, it's the right thing to do. If you feel like bullying is affecting your grades, making you skip school, causing damage to your property, or making you feel unsafe, you *need* to tell someone—a parent, a teacher you trust, or a school official.

Uh-oh... Are You a Bully?

Sometimes you can become a bully without even realizing it. Maybe you started making fun of someone with your friends at the lunch table one day. You all laughed—and it didn't *seem* like the person noticed. But then your teasing became more obvious and more frequent. Eventually you got to the point where you thought that some people didn't have feelings. That they didn't matter.

But if you're treating others in a way you wouldn't want to be treated, you are being a bully. It's not funny. It's not harmless. It's cruel. Or maybe you're just one of the innocent bystanders. Sure, your friends might pick on people, but you don't participate. You watch it happen, but you're not really doing anything *wrong*. Right?

Not quite. Katrina told me that in high school, 25 percent of girls are being bullied.[3] From everyone I've talked to, it seems that only 15 percent do the bullying. That leaves 60 percent of us in the middle, choosing to either do nothing *or* stand up for what's right. Sure, it's easiest to ignore bullying and just not do anything. After all, if we did say something, people might turn on us.

Yep, it's scary to stand up for someone being bullied. But it's what Jesus did. Again and again and again. And once you stand up, it's likely others who have witnessed the bullying and feel the same way you do will have the courage to speak up. Maybe voicing your opinion will make it easier for others to follow along.

I wish I could tell you I always stood up for the kid getting picked on. But I didn't. And the main reason was peer pressure from my friends. It's a pretty embarrassing story, but I'll tell you about it in the next chapter.

Chapter 7

Once upon a Yellow-and-Pink-Checkered Jacket
(What to Do About Peer Pressure)

In high school, after I moved to Odyssey, I hung out with two friends, Blaire and Carla, who were pretty popular. After my experiences in junior high, it felt awesome to get attention from the "in" crowd. They were really nice to me . . . but not always to everyone else. They'd often make fun of kids who dressed like "dorks" or "nerds," as they called them. I'd kind of smile when they started making fun of those kids. But one day, the harm these words could cause hit me head-on.

We were at the mall and caught sight of Larry Melwood. Larry was a supernice guy, and I really liked him, but he did dress in high-water pants and wore nerdy glasses.

"Did you notice his pocket protector with like a billion pens in it?" Blaire joked.

"And the roll of tape holding his glasses together," Carla added.

Blaire and Carla laughed. I didn't.

"So what are you saying?" I said. "Just because he looks a little funny, you don't want to talk with him."

The laughing stopped, and Blaire and Carla stared at me. Both of them pressured me to make fun of him a little bit.

"Say it," they kept telling me. "He's . . . a . . . geek."

And, eventually, I did. In fact, I ended up saying it louder than I intended.

"Larry Melwood is a geek!"

The worst part is Larry had come back around to say hi to me and heard my words loud and clear! He ran off before I could explain. And, really, how *could* I explain?*

I'd done something I didn't want to do. Something I didn't believe in. And the only reason I'd said anything was because my friends pressured me. What a dumb excuse.

---

* For the whole story, listen to "With a Little Help from My Friends," episode 348, album 27, *The Search for Whit*.

Pressure Points

But that's how peer pressure works. Years ago I helped Whit and Jason go through a bunch of clothes, books, and other stuff to decide what to donate. Jason pulled out this awful yellow-and-pink-checkered jacket. We all laughed when he tried it on.

"Whit, did you really wear that?" I asked.

He chuckled. "Everyone was wearing this style at the time. My friends told me it looked great, and for some reason I believed them."

After we finished packing everything up, Jason and I took some of Whit's old clothes to a local charity.

"Can you imagine all those guys walking around in ridiculous-looking jackets?" I said. "The things we do just because everybody else is doing it."

"And it's not just silly-looking fashions, Connie," Jason said.

Later, at Whit's End, we connected with my mom to talk more about the dangers of peer pressure. Jason admitted he got in trouble in high school a couple of times just because he didn't know how to say no to his friends' destructive ideas. My mom shared about a situation she had at work when she agreed with her fellow employees about an idea their boss had—despite knowing it was the wrong decision.

"Peer pressure can make us do things that are out of character no matter how old we are," Jason said. "But I've also been in situations where pressure from my peers helped me make a good decision."

Jason was right. There *are* different types of peer pressure:

Good peer pressure is when friends pressure us to do positive things or to try something we might not do on our own. Like when I was nervous about running for student council, and my friends rallied around me to tell me that I'd be great at it.

"The school needs you," they said. "You should definitely run."

All those words felt like pressure, but it was good pressure because I needed the encouragement to go for it.

Silent peer pressure is what you feel when you look around and notice that all your friends are wearing the same shoes—the ones you don't have. So you feel pressure to get them. This happens with clothes, hairstyles, where to sit in class, who you should talk to in school, and even what kind of soda you drink. Silent peer pressure causes us to blend in with everyone else.

Dangerous peer pressure is the pressure that can get us into real trouble. This is the kind of pressure that makes us do things we know are wrong. Watching the horror movie at the slumber party even though we know it will give us nightmares. Shoplifting the lip gloss from the supermarket and potentially getting charged with a crime. Cheating on a test, smoking a cigarette, trying alcohol, or even announcing in the mall that Larry Melwood is a geek.

"Well, not all those things are dangerous," you might say. But anything that goes against what you believe and who you are (remember those lists back in chapter 1?) puts you in danger, because you're heading in a direction that's *not* you. If you give in to your friends one time, it will be even easier to do it again. And again. And again. Somehow that "only this once" promise you made to yourself has taken you further than you ever imagined it would.

Every addiction or bad habit starts with a first time or an "only once" mentality. Ask any alcoholic, compulsive liar, shoplifter, or smoker. None of them intended for that first choice to become a regular part of their lives, but that's always where it starts.

When I asked some girls at Whit's End why they didn't speak up against peer pressure, they said . . .

- "If I didn't go along with it, I knew they would start teasing me."
- "I didn't really like the cool girls, but I liked the idea of being invited to the cool parties."
- "I was worried about what other people would say about me behind my back—or how they would judge me."

And they're not alone. When we're going through our teen years, we're at an age where caring what people think about us is at an all-time high. It's hard to go against the crowd. But it's not impossible.

Taking *This* Moment to Prepare for *That* Moment

Peer pressure can show up when you least expect it. Maybe it's the pressure to share your answers on a homework assignment with a friend or to buy trendy clothes—even though they're really overpriced. At some point, you'll likely be pressured to drink, smoke, use drugs, or pair up as a couple, which can lead to even more pressure to experiment with behaviors you'll likely regret.

Now I know what you're thinking. *Connie, I wouldn't do that. I've heard how that stuff is dangerous and causes disease and all sorts of problems. I'm not stupid.*

I know you're not stupid, but even the smartest girls can give in under pressure. We can be so concerned with being liked, or afraid that our friends won't want to hang out with us anymore if we act like a goody-goody, that we end up trying things we know are bad for us. So even though at *this* moment, you'd say, "I'd never start drinking alcohol," in *that* moment, when your friends are all looking at you, you might have second thoughts. Decide now not only that you're *going* to avoid destructive behaviors but also *how* you're going to do it.

You have to make a plan. Because when you're in that moment and everybody's saying it's cool, you might not know how to respond. Think ahead of time about why you don't want to smoke or drink or play kissing games or take part in mean pranks on other kids. Then when other kids say, "C'mon, don't be such a loser. It'll be fun!" or "All of us are doing it!" or "Are you a baby or something?" you can respond in a mature way.

Some girls have the courage to flat-out say, "It's wrong because that's what the Bible says," or "I'm choosing to obey my parents." But sometimes we need to be prepared with additional reasons to convince our friends to leave us alone.

For drugs, alcohol, and cigarettes, you might say . . .

- "My health is superimportant to me, and it's just not worth it."
- "I've seen that stuff mess up too many people's lives, so I don't even want to try it."
- "Too many girls do dumb things when they're drunk or high. I don't want to end up on YouTube."

For bullying or picking on someone, you might say . . .

- "I feel guilty when I pick on people."
- "I've been on the receiving end of getting picked on, and I decided a long time ago that I don't want to be a part of it."
- "Bullying hurts people too much. I just don't want to go there."

For shoplifting, graffiti, or breaking the law, you might say . . .

- "Maybe I am a chicken. But that's better than being a jailbird."
- "It's not worth how long I'd be grounded."

- "I just don't see how that's any fun. How about if we . . . [suggest another activity]?"

Of course, there are plenty of other areas where you might feel pressured to go against your beliefs. So before you enter a potentially pressure-packed situation—a party, sleepover, school dance, or concert—be prepared with what you're going to say *and* come up with a plan for how you're going to release the pressure.

In many of these situations, having a good friend with you can be powerful. If you've chosen a best friend who shares your values, it's a whole lot easier to stand up to a crowd when she's there to stand by you. Make a pact with your core group of friends that you'll support each other if you find yourselves in a situation where you're feeling the pressure to cave in and go against your convictions.

It's also a great idea to have an open conversation with your parents about what to do when you feel pressured. They probably had to get out of sticky situations when they were younger and can give you some wise advice. Ask if you can call them to come get you from a party or sleepover without worrying that you might get in trouble for what's going on there. Parents know what it's like to go through the teen years. They want what's best for you and will likely be happy to help you get out of any situation you find yourself in.

Here's a Secret...

Olivia told me about this top-secret plan she has with her family. If she's ever in an uncomfortable situation or one where she's feeling pressure, she texts her mom the letters CMX, which means "Call me with an excuse." A few minutes later, her phone rings, and her mom tells her to come home right away. That way Olivia is able to get out of the situation easily. You might talk to your parents about setting up a text or phone system too. It's always better to be prepared—just in case!

Audience of One

Let me finish this chapter by getting back to when I made fun of Larry in the mall. I did end up apologizing to him. And the next time Carla and Blaire started making fun of someone, I stood up to my friends and said I didn't want to be someone who makes fun of the "Larrys of this world."

That pretty much ended our friendship. Although it was disappointing to lose my popular friends, I realized those weren't the friends I wanted to have anyway.

Mr. Whittaker used to tell me, "You plus Jesus makes a majority." He meant that even if I felt ganged up on, God was on my side. I like that. What God thinks about me is more important than what everybody in my school thinks—even the popular kids.

William Shakespeare wrote, "All the world's a stage." People are always looking at us and *judging* our performance. By following Whit's advice, I started living like there was only one Person in the audience. As Christ followers, that's how we should all live. In Galatians 1:10 the apostle Paul said, "Obviously, I'm not trying to win the approval of people, but of God. If pleasing people were my goal, I would not be Christ's servant" (NLT).

Knowing our lives please God is way better than anything our friends can offer us. Besides, pleasing people may cause us to do something we'd never do otherwise—like wear a yellow-and-pink-checkered jacket.

Just ask Whit.

Your Turn

Practice *this* day what you'll do when *that* day comes and you're tempted to go along with the crowd. So what would you do if . . .

1. You spent a couple of hours last night reading your history assignment and answering some questions. When you get to class today, Cassie and Noel ask to copy your answers. They were too busy to do it themselves. Cassie looks at you with

puppy-dog eyes, while Noel says, "You don't want us to fail, do you?" So you say . . .

2. You're at a big sleepover at a friend's house. One of the girls finds an open bottle of wine in the refrigerator. The host's parents are already asleep. "We should try some," your friend says. "Okay," your host says, "but not too much. I don't want my parents to find out." What do you do?

3. You go to the movies with two of your friends. When you walk in, three boys from your school are waiting there. Your two friends start holding hands with two of the boys. That leaves just you and Gavin looking awkwardly at each other. In the theater, the two boys put their arms around your friends. Gavin tries to put his arm around you. So you . . .

Chapter 8

Blame It on My Hippocampus

(How to Make Good Decisions)

"Connie, what were you thinking!?"

My mom asked me that after I thought it would be fun for my friends and me to move our living-room furniture into the backyard so we could hang out under the stars. It was fun—until a rainstorm came through and drenched the couches.

Mom asked me that same question after I spent all the money I was saving for a car on a pair of boots I saw in a store window.

Then there was the time I signed up to coach a church-league youth basketball team when I'd never been that good at basketball. And, well, a *lot* of other times.

They all seemed like really good ideas . . . until they didn't.

But at least now I know why. See, by middle school, we have almost-adult-sized brains, but they're still not completely developed.[1] Eugene explained it to me once, but he threw around words like *synapses* and *frontal cortex*, so I'll try to make it a little easier to understand.

Our brains have lots of parts. Think of your mind as a group of townspeople, each in charge of different functions—balance, movement, memory, emotions, speaking, and a variety of other things. Then there's the mayor, the hippocampus. Mayor Hippocampus is the *self-regulatory center*. That means it reasons and determines whether an idea makes sense or not. The challenge is that the hippocampus isn't completely developed until you're around age twenty-four.[2]

So teens and preteens have big brains and fully developed emotions. When you add in hormones that bounce around like termites on a trampoline, it's extra challenging for teens, because the emotions in their brains can talk a lot louder than logic. So in my case, the thought *An outdoor living room under the stars would be so much fun!* drowned out any logic about the forecast calling for rain, and our couches not being waterproof.

See how this imbalance between reason and emotion can cause problems?

The imbalance makes us more interested in an immediate reward (I'm dying to buy these cute jeans) than in a long-term benefit (I could save for college). And sometimes that imbalance makes us react emotionally without first thinking things through.

Battling the Blurts

A listener to my *Candid Conversations with Connie* radio show asked me this question:

> **Q:** Everyone tells me that honesty is the best policy. If that's true, why do I get in trouble for being disrespectful when I express my honest opinion?

I could've answered her with a verse from the Bible: "There is more hope for a fool than for someone who speaks without thinking" (Proverbs 29:20, NLT). But I thought about it and answered her with this story instead:

Whit and I were driving back to Whit's End after picking up some supplies. I was filling him in on my latest sundae creation (FYI—popcorn, peanut, and fudge sundaes are as good as they sound).

Suddenly I interrupted myself with a scream. "Aaack! Watch out for the wagon!"

A little red wagon rolled down a grassy hill—right in front of our car! Whit screeched on the brakes and tried to swerve, but we still hit the wagon with a loud clunk. As Whit pulled over to check for damage, an angry man came running toward us.

"Why weren't you driving more carefully?" he shouted. "What's wrong with you people? You've ruined my wagon! You shouldn't even have a driver's license!"

He was saying more stuff, but at this point I was yelling back at him. I mean, really, it was completely unfair of him to blame us for his wagon running into the road!

Somewhere in the middle of my shouting that he was the most irresponsible wagon owner I'd ever met, Whit put his hand on my shoulder and whispered in my ear, "I think you need to calm down."

He was right, of course. I wasn't doing anyone any good by screaming at that man. Once I took a deep breath and got myself under control, we respectfully discussed what happened and cleared everything up. I felt pretty silly getting back into the car, because I shouldn't have flown off the handle like I did. But as we pulled away from the curb, Whit told me something I'll never forget: "I felt the same way you did, Connie."

"Really?" I said. "I didn't think you ever got mad."

Whit chuckled. "Our thoughts might be the same, but the difference is the space between my brain and my mouth. It's usually not wise to blurt out emotional reactions."

As I grew older, I saw the wisdom in that advice. But my blurts—based on my honest thoughts and feelings—didn't stop completely. I said some pretty mean things to my mom when I was feeling especially angry. And I once told Eugene I never wanted to see him again after he beat me at checkers six times in a row.

Maybe I've learned a few lessons along the way, or it could be that my hippocampus finally grew up. Now I'm less likely to blurt out stuff in the moment, and I'm more likely to think things through.

Feeding the Hippocampus

Understanding that your brain isn't fully developed doesn't give you an excuse for anything. So don't try to install a skylight in your basement bedroom and then simply explain to your angry parents, "Blame it on my undeveloped hippocampus."

You can avoid being ruled by emotions and the bad decisions that follow by trying these ideas:

1. *Give yourself some time.* Don't make a split-second decision based on feelings, like "Sure, I'll take that puppy"; "I think I'll paint my room black. Mom won't mind"; or "I'm quitting the gymnastics team—it's way too hard!" Step away from the excitement, hurt, or anger you're feeling. Give yourself some time to think through the decision without intense emotions coloring the process. Two hours later, ask yourself, "Is this still a good idea?"

2. *Go to your parents.* Ask them about their thoughts on a decision you're thinking about. Do they think your schedule can handle another activity? Do they think it's petty to end a friendship because of some gossip that started about you? Just talking about it might make the decision more clear.

3. *Pray about it.* God wants to give you wisdom. James 1:5 tells us clearly, "If you need wisdom, ask our generous God, and he will give it to you" (NLT). If you take the time to sit with God and tell Him what you're struggling with, you might start feeling a tug on your heart toward the right thing.

4. *Interview the problem.* Write these questions down and refer to them when you're uncertain: Is this healthy for my mind and body? Will it hurt anyone else? Would I do it if my grandma was watching? Does this go against anything the

Bible tells me? In a month, will I regret it? What are the pros and cons? By answering these questions, you'll get a better idea of what you should do.

The Upside . . .

Having an underdeveloped hippocampus isn't all bad. You're more likely to try something new. While some adults overanalyze a decision or get intimidated by a new opportunity, teens tend to have a "Let's just do it!" attitude. You're also often more enthusiastic when it comes to participating in projects that help people, like missions trips or volunteering.

Another benefit is that a developing brain is still moldable. Think of your brain as wet cement. You're at a time when you can learn new things and form good habits that will last a lifetime. For example, when you make the choice to eat healthy now, your body grows accustomed to reaching for carrots instead of cupcakes. You form good habits that carry on for decades, resulting in a healthy weight, more energy, and an overall more fulfilling life.

The Downside . . .

But that "wet cement" can also develop some negative—even deadly—habits that will eventually be set in stone. Did you know that 80 percent of adult smokers started the habit as teens?[3]

It's very likely that in the next few years, you'll be presented with the opportunity to smoke cigarettes, drink alcohol, use illegal drugs, or misuse prescription drugs. Maybe you're already surrounded by kids who are doing those things, and you might think, *Well, they're enjoying it, so what's the harm in trying it once?*

We already talked about peer pressure in the last chapter and how you need to know *before* you get into a situation who you are and what you're going to do. But it's good to know that the reason you may fear rejection so much right now is because of your still-developing brain. The sensible words of Mayor Hippocampus are often drowned out by your emotions.

One way to get your emotions under control is to calmly and thoroughly examine good information. Your friends who are smokers or drug users will tell you how something makes them *feel*, but they won't give you all the facts.

What Your Friends Won't Tell You

Olivia told me she has a friend who smokes electronic cigarettes and said they were "safe." Olivia wanted to know this:

Q: Are e-cigarettes better for you than regular cigarettes?

Here's the scoop on smoking either electronic cigarettes (often called e-cigarettes or e-cigs) or tobacco-filled paper ones—there is no "better." Both can be described by another B word: B-A-D!

E-cigarettes

While electronic cigarettes aren't filled with tobacco and awful tar, most e-cigs still release some nicotine, which is addictive and can harm your heart. Eugene researched this for me and found out that in addition to nicotine, e-cigarettes can affect the smoker with chemicals like *tetramethylpyrazine*, *nitrosamines*, and *diethylene glycol*. (Personally, I don't know much about chemistry. But science words with syllables that include *meth*, *nitro*, and *die* really scare me.) Eugene said that these chemicals have been linked to cancer and other health problems.

One more thing: e-cigarettes are "smokeless." They have a little battery-charged heater that warms up a liquid. Instead of smelly smoke, an e-cig releases water vapor, which doesn't stink up your clothes, breath, and hair. But that just makes e-cigs easier to hide from parents and teachers.

Want to hear something really dumb? E-cigarettes were designed to help adults *stop* smoking, but they're actually encouraging teens to *start*. Some young people, like Olivia's friend, think e-cigs are cool, safe, and fun. The fact that e-cigs come in fruit flavors makes them seem as harmless as candy. But they're not. Anything with nicotine is highly addictive. Many kids who start smoking e-cigs begin smoking real cigarettes.[4] That's the opposite of what was supposed to happen.

Tobacco Cigarettes

If someone begins smoking tobacco cigarettes, it's like jumping into an alligator-infested swimming pool. You're pretty much asking for trouble. Cigarette smoking leads to more than ten kinds of cancer![5] But there are immediate negative physical effects as well. Your breath smells terrible. Your lung capacity decreases, which means you won't be able to do some of the physical activities you enjoy. Short-term use of cigarettes will cause your teeth to turn yellow and wrinkles to form around your mouth. A chronic cough could develop even after smoking for a short time. None of these things are very cool.

Drugs

Many studies show that smoking cigarettes can lead you down a path to taking other drugs. Teens who start smoking are way more likely to try illegal drugs. How likely? One study showed that twelve- to fifteen-year-olds who smoked cigarettes were 44 percent more likely to try crack (a form of cocaine).[6]

Here's a Secret...

I made some bad choices before I was a Christian—things I really regret now. For a long time, I thought God must think less of me because of those behaviors. But then I remembered a piece of a Bible verse that goes something like this: "As far as the east is from the west, so far has God removed our sins from us"* God sees me as pure and holy.

If you're a Christian and have made some bad choices, know this: God doesn't see you as any less valuable. He loves you—period! Even when you mess up a thousand times. Don't let the lies of Satan tell you otherwise. Of course, this doesn't mean you should keep making the same poor choices over and over again. First, ask God for forgiveness, and then ask Him to give you the strength to make better decisions going forward.

We'll never be perfect. The best we can do is try every day to make our next choice a good one.

---

* Connie remembered part of Psalm 103:12 and put it in her own words.

Crack is only one drug on a long list that may be offered to you. Meth, spice, marijuana, hallucinogenic mushrooms, and prescription drugs are also popular among some groups. But remember this: *all* illegal drugs are harmful. No matter how safe someone insists a drug is, you don't know how it'll affect you. People have died after the first time they tried cocaine. Plus, you can't control how addictive a drug may be. Even after trying a drug only once, you can develop a craving for more. (Imagine a feeling that's five times stronger than a chocolate craving, and that's just part of the picture.)

Another thing to keep in mind is that like e-cigs, the vast majority of illegal drugs aren't regulated by the government. In other words, you really have no idea what's in them.

Food products you buy in the grocery store are required to list their ingredients. Foods made in your school cafeteria go through regular inspections and meet certain requirements. But the people who make illegal drugs aren't interested in your health or the quality of their product. They're interested in your money. That means they'll add dangerous chemicals, especially ones that increase the addictiveness of the drug. You don't know who formulated them, or what they added. What you can be certain of is this: they're not worth the risk!

Alcohol

Alcohol advertisements often show people drinking, laughing, and having a good time. But they don't show anyone tripping over the coffee table because she can't walk, throwing up on the front lawn, or shaving her head because she thinks—at the time—it's a great idea.

Nope, drinking alcohol doesn't make you glamorous. In fact, it can be especially dangerous for girls. Because you have a smaller frame and weigh less, even one drink can quickly impact your system. It slows down your brain, inhibiting your ability to reason and greatly increasing the likelihood of having an accident (anything from a car crash to falling down the stairs). Things you would never imagine doing suddenly don't seem so bad when you have alcohol in your system. Because teen brains are still developing, alcohol and drugs will cause far more damage to you than they do in adults—and it's not good for them, either.

Penny's Story

I had a friend in high school—Shelia—who was amazing! She could make prize-winning peanut brittle and balance a cat on her head—at the same time. She was also an all-star basketball player and a straight-A student. But one night at a party, she decided she'd have a couple of drinks. It didn't seem like a big deal at the time, because she hardly felt any different. But driving home that night, she got into an accident. She broke her arm, so she missed playing in the championship basketball game, not to mention wrecking her parents' car—and their trust in her. The next day, when I went to give her a get-well bouquet of celery stalks (they were on sale), she was really scared. She knew her accident could have been so much worse. She even could have killed someone!

Fortunately, when it comes to *most* bad decisions, we can fix them, learn from them, and move on. Even those rain-drenched couches could be brought back inside and dried off (although I always thought they smelled a little funny). But when it comes to issues like alcohol and drugs, those decisions often come with far more serious consequences. A single bad decision really can wreck your life. It could even mean life and death.

I know drugs and alcohol are pretty heavy topics for a book with a fun picnic on the cover, but I wanted to talk about this because it's that important. Like Olivia, you may have friends who use these substances, and naturally you're curious. If you have any questions or concerns about drugs, alcohol, or cigarettes, make sure to talk to your parents about them.

Your Turn

There's an old saying that goes like this: "If you don't stand for something, you will fall for anything." Take some time right now to decide what you'd like your teen years to stand for. Review the decision-making suggestions in the "Feeding the Hippocampus" section of this chapter:

1. Give yourself some time.
2. Go to your parents.
3. Pray about it.
4. Interview the problem.

Then take some time to ask yourself questions like these: What are my long-term goals? How much do my emotions shut down Mayor Hippocampus, and how can I make sure I'm making good choices? How can I use my young, enthusiastic brain to make a difference for God?

Here's some space to write down your thoughts:

_____

_____

CANDID CONVERSATIONS WITH CONNIE, VOL. 2

Chapter 9

Tapping into Your Superpower

(Skills for Surviving... and Thriving)

During high school, I agreed to substitute as the school's mascot at a football game. I dressed up in a big owl costume, complete with a giant—and heavy—stuffed head. Everything went fine until halftime when I needed to use the restroom. The head wouldn't fit in the stall. When I tried to take it off, I couldn't. It had somehow gotten stuck in my hair! Thankfully, I was able to find Ashley in the stands and ask her to help. She couldn't make it budge either. It took two janitors, a crowbar, and a pair of scissors to rescue me from living the rest of my life as a bird. By the time they got off the head, Ashley and I were laughing so hard that tears were running down our faces.

Between peer pressure, cliques, and mean girls, I've probably made you a little uneasy about growing up. Sorry 'bout that. But here's a bit of hope: As many challenges as you'll have during your teen years, you'll likely have even more absolutely amazing moments. Friendships will grow deeper. Laughter will get bigger. Learning will become more interesting. Trying new things will get wackier (especially if you become a mascot). You'll form inside jokes with close friends, experience amazing adventures, and create fun memories.

So here's another question for your notebook (remember the one you made in chapter 1?): *What has been one of your most enjoyable moments?*

Maybe one of them was laughing so hard at the lunch table with your friends that milk came out your nose. Or getting your first hit on the softball team. Or going on a long bike ride with your dad. Or a week at camp with your youth group. Or studying hard for that science test and getting an A. Or being awarded first chair in band. Or the compliment you received on your art project. Or completing that long run. Or a perfect sunset over the ocean on a family vacation.

When you have those happy moments, jot them down. Remember them. Look back at them when it feels like life is beating you up.

Don't let the not-so-great days keep you from appreciating the gift of the good moments. It's likely that something will go wrong every day, but it's also very likely that something will go right. Notice those things. Relish them. And say a prayer of thanks.

When you focus on the beautiful moments—the gifts of what you have instead of the lack of what you don't have—your mood will improve. And when you're feeling better about your life, you're going to be friendlier and more upbeat. It's not magic. It's a choice. And it's in the Bible. First Thessalonians 5:16-18 says to "be joyful always" and "give thanks in all circumstances, for this is God's will for you in Christ Jesus." But you have to *choose* to be joyful and thankful.

Try, Try Again

You also have to choose to break out of your comfort zone. You won't grow and develop new talents unless you take some risks. The girls in my Wednesday-night Bible study recently had a bunch of questions about growing up. So I thought I'd share some of them and give you my answers. Here's one from Taryn:

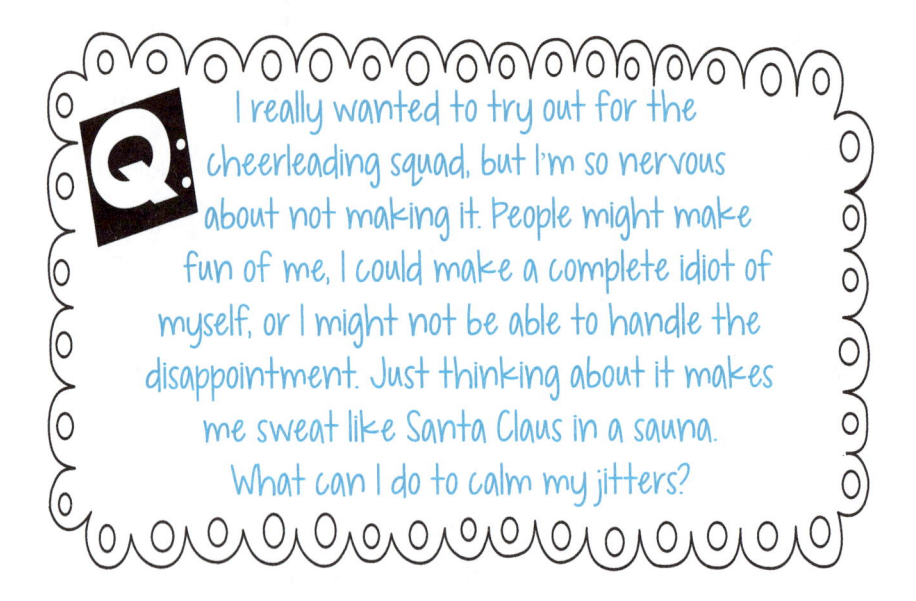

> **Q:** I really wanted to try out for the cheerleading squad, but I'm so nervous about not making it. People might make fun of me, I could make a complete idiot of myself, or I might not be able to handle the disappointment. Just thinking about it makes me sweat like Santa Claus in a sauna. What can I do to calm my jitters?

First of all, Taryn, put on some antiperspirant. Second, put on some perspective. Don't make choices based on your fears. The Bible tells us in 2 Timothy 1:7 that "God has not given us a spirit of fear and timidity, but of power, love, and self-discipline" (NLT).

You don't need to be afraid. God has given you His strength, showered you with His unconditional love, and gifted you with the ability to work hard. So *practice* before you try out! God doesn't promise you success, but He *will* give you the courage to try your best. And all you can do is give your best.

Olivia has a great story about this.

Olivia's Story

I really wanted to audition for the school play *You're a Good Man, Charlie Brown*. But I knew that a lot of older kids who had more experience would be auditioning too. I convinced myself I didn't have a chance, so why bother? But on the day of auditions, a friend of mine convinced me to audition with her. That did make it a little easier. When we walked into the auditorium, it was packed with people watching. I immediately envisioned them pelting me with rotten fruit or bursting out in laughter at my sad attempt at playing Lucy. I was two seconds from running out the door when the drama instructor called my name. I squeezed my hands to keep them from shaking and went ahead with the audition.

First thing the next morning, I hurried to where the cast list had been posted and discovered . . . I hadn't made it. For sure I was disappointed, but not as much as I thought I would be. A lot of kids hadn't made the cast, and they were already talking about being involved in designing sets, creating programs, and working on costumes. A few of them asked me to be on their committees. I ended up working on the makeup team. The drama instructor noticed how hard I worked. She complimented me on my audition and gave me a few pointers for my next tryout. (She wanted me to audition again!) Since then, I've been in several school plays. Sometimes onstage. Other times, behind the scenes. But I've never regretted that first audition, even though it seemed like a failure. I learned a lot from it, met a bunch of new friends, and discovered some talents that I didn't know I had.

Your Turn

Here's an exercise for you. Think of one thing you want to do that you're scared of. It might be as simple as pursuing a friendship with a girl in your class. Or it might be running for class president. Whatever it is, write it down below:

Now list three to five reasons you want to do it. For example, if your activity is trying out for the basketball team, these might be reasons you'd want to do it:

- Because it's good exercise
- To make some new friends
- Because I really have fun playing basketball
- Because I enjoy competition and the excitement of the games
- Because I like being part of a team and belonging to something

_____

_____

_____

Last, put down the reasons you're afraid to go for it:

_____

_____

Often, there's only one drawback of trying out for things: "I'll be disappointed or embarrassed if I don't make it." But even trying out for something and not making it can be good for you. My mom told me that once, and I said, "Augh, Mom! Don't tell me stuff like that." So now you can say to me, "Augh, Connie! Don't tell me stuff like that." I didn't like hearing it, but it's true. Every time I tried out for something or stretched myself by doing an activity I was interested in, I became a better, more well-rounded person. I was proud of myself, even if I didn't make it.

Beating Life's Embarrassments

I hope that helps, Taryn. Now here's a question from Paytin:

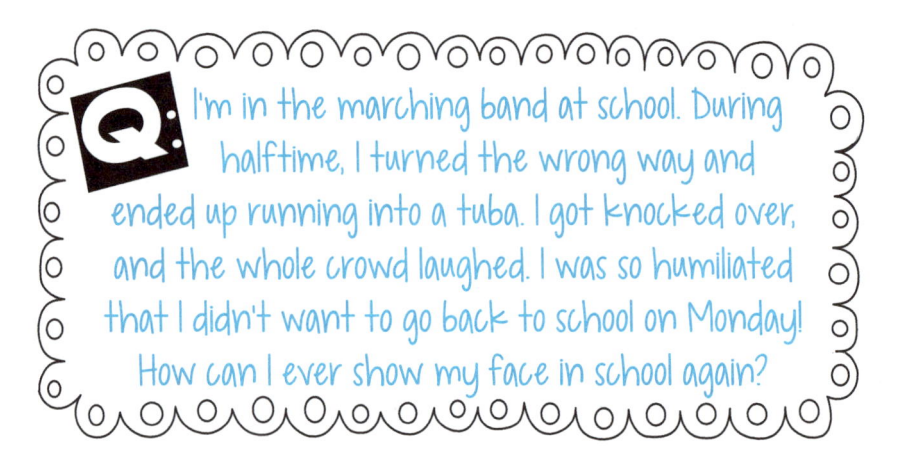

> **Q:** I'm in the marching band at school. During halftime, I turned the wrong way and ended up running into a tuba. I got knocked over, and the whole crowd laughed. I was so humiliated that I didn't want to go back to school on Monday! How can I ever show my face in school again?

Ah, Paytin, if I skipped school over every embarrassing incident I've had, well . . . I'd still be in fifth grade. We all have events we'd like to forget, but none of them are as bad as we make them out to be. Just like seeing our zits as bigger than anyone else sees them, we see our embarrassing moments as more humiliating. Sure, some people might tease you, but eventually you'll probably laugh about it too. Or at least not cringe every time you think about it. To help you feel a little better, some of the girls shared an embarrassing story:

Penny: We were lining up to get on the bus after a field trip to a museum, when a giant bird swooped over us. Suddenly I felt something goopy land on my head. Yep, that bird had left its mark. Everyone laughed. I had to get on the bus, sit by myself (for obvious reasons), and ride the whole half hour back to school with bird droppings stuck in my hair. Yuck.

Tamika: During a softball game, I was running to home plate after a teammate hit a ball way into the outfield. Our team was winning by a lot, and I was feeling pretty good about it. So I did a little victory spin as I rounded third base. But I tripped over my own feet and ended up spraining my ankle! Not only did I get tagged out, but I also made a complete fool of myself in front of the whole crowd!

Olivia: Okay, I still sleep with a stuffed duck that I had as a baby. On the Monday after a weekend slumber party, my best friend shouted at me in a completely crowded hallway, "Olivia! You left your ducky-wucky at my house! I have it in my locker." For weeks people called me ducky-wucky.

Katrina: In eighth grade, this boy I had a crush on came up to my lunch table and asked about an upcoming assignment. I attempted to appear cool and relaxed, so I casually started to blow a bubble with a piece of gum I was chewing. Unfortunately, I blew too hard (likely because I was so nervous) and blew the gum out of my mouth and onto his nose! He never asked me about class assignments again.

Camilla: I won a contest at school and got to give the daily announcements over the intercom. But before I started, I asked the school secretary if she could wait a minute because "I really, *really* need to go to the bathroom." Unfortunately, the intercom was already turned on, and the entire school heard my announcement.

So, Paytin, everybody has lived through embarrassing moments (including the people who tease you). But remember, the quicker you can laugh about it, the quicker you'll get over it. And others will tire of teasing you about it. It's all part of growing up. Think of it this way: It'll give you a great story to tell!

And you can always remind yourself of Isaiah 54:4: "Do not be afraid; you will not suffer shame. Do not fear disgrace; you will not be humiliated. You will forget the shame of your youth."

Phew . . . that's good news for me!

The Chicken or the Egg . . .

The questions from my Bible-study group kept coming. This one is from Jillian:

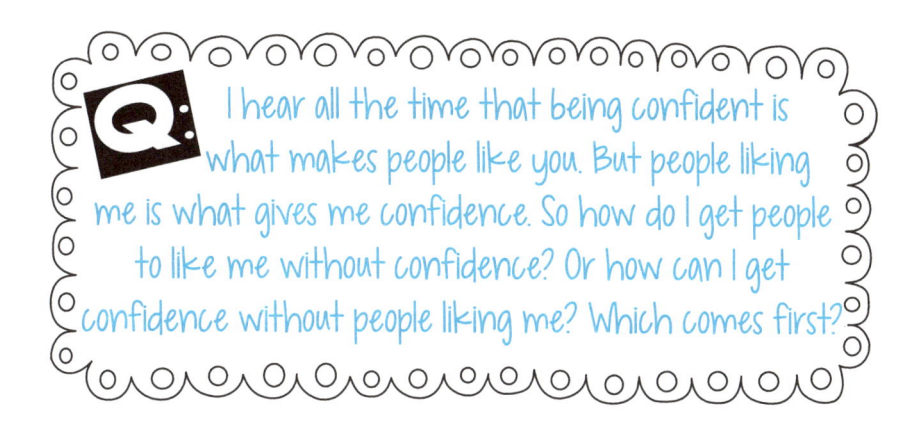

> **Q:** I hear all the time that being confident is what makes people like you. But people liking me is what gives me confidence. So how do I get people to like me without confidence? Or how can I get confidence without people liking me? Which comes first?

You really should meet my friend Wooton. I'm guessing you two think the same way.

First, Jillian, it's true that people are often drawn to someone who is confident. We may think that we have to be beautiful, supertalented, or athletic, or have some amazing superpower for people to like us. But the most admired people are often those who just feel comfortable in their own skin. In other words, they like who they are.

It's hard to say what comes first, but try this tip: *fake confidence to make confidence.* Really. If you don't feel it, just fake it for a while. Convince yourself that you're superconfident. Try standing taller, practice walking with better posture, and look people in the eyes. Act like you know you're somebody important—because you are! Smile more, even at people you don't know well. Say hi, start a conversation, speak up in class, join a club, take a risk that only a person who was really confident would.

Here's a Secret...

The truth is, people care less about how you look or what you do and care more about what you think of *them*. People like to be liked. But not in a gushy, insincere way. They want you to care about what they think, listen to their thoughts and opinions, ask them questions about their lives, and genuinely compliment them.

I once was at a party where I was supernervous. This guy walked up to me and started talking about his job. He was a penguin keeper at the zoo. I thought it was really interesting to hear about penguins—how you tell them apart, what they eat, if he'd learned penguin language. So I asked a few questions, but mostly he did the talking. Later, when I was leaving, I overheard him talking to someone about me. "Did you meet Connie Kendall?" he said. "She is such a great conversationalist!" I almost laughed out loud. Because I hadn't even talked that much. I'd just listened and been interested!

Another key to confidence is to treat yourself like someone worth treasuring. Catch yourself when you start saying critical words to yourself and turn them to compliments. Instead of berating yourself for how bushy your eyebrows are, or how dumb your answer was in history class, give yourself grace. Remind yourself of the beautiful and positive things about yourself. Take time to pamper yourself: do your nails, take a warm bath, read a great book. You're worth it!

Top Survival Tips

The Bible-study girls had lots of other questions, but I want to end with this one from Reagan:

> **Q: What's the best advice for surviving the teen years?**

That's a great question, Reagan. I'm going to let some of the girls chime in on that one.

> OLIVIA: Find something you're passionate about. If school is rough for you, look for an activity outside of school. I began doing drama productions at Whit's End. A cousin of mine got really involved at a dance school. My little sister started taking horseback-riding lessons. Becoming more active in your church youth group can be a lifesaver too. You'll be introduced to a whole new circle of friends who don't have the same ideas about you as the kids at school, and you'll feel better about yourself when you're involved in something that energizes you.

KATRINA: I recommend every teenager find a mentor who's just a few years older. Perhaps a former babysitter or an older girl at your church. If you recall my story, my friend Joleen was an immense help. She'd recently been through what I was experiencing and could offer advice and encouragement. These are the girls you can call when you're not sure what to do.

The advice I always give is to volunteer for an organization you believe in. It's easy to become self-absorbed. (I'm talking from personal experience here.) But the more you think about yourself, the more obsessed you'll become about how you look, how you compare to others, and what people think of you. Not exactly healthy thoughts. But if you regularly volunteer at something that matters to you, it gives you a bigger purpose in life. Plus, people who volunteer are generally happier. So take a Saturday shift at the dog shelter, start working with children with disabilities, or organize a group at your church to feed Sunday lunches to the homeless. Not only will this give you more purpose in life, but it also can make you more grateful for all you have. That will help you survive the teen years.

Now that we've talked about some of the terrible and wonderful things that can happen with friends, nonfriends, and cliques, as well as how to overcome embarrassing moments, there's a whole other part of the population that we should chat about. You guessed it . . . boys!

Chapter 10

How to Survive Mad Cow Disease

(The Laws of Like)

I sat in Whit's office, breathing heavily and listing my symptoms: "Difficulty walking, trouble breathing, dry mouth, profuse sweating, struggling to form words, flushed skin, racing heart . . ." Surely, I was dying.

Eugene typed my symptoms into a medical website. "Apparently, Miss Kendall, you either have mad cow disease, a brain infection, typhoid fever, or a vitamin B12 deficiency."

"I don't think it's any of those things," I said.

"Well, then, Connie," Eugene continued. "Perhaps you're in love."

My face turned even more red. Standing up, I went to find Whit for a second opinion.

"Well, maybe it's not quite love," Whit told me when I found him downstairs. "But it might be some serious 'like.' "

Earlier that day, I'd been introduced to Robert Mitchell. Correction: make that stunning-green-eyes, amazing-voice, smile-that-melts-you, perfectly-charming, helped-me-carry-heavy-boxes-with-the-greatest-of-ease Robert Mitchell (aka Mitch). When I first laid eyes on him, my stomach did this funny flip, my heart sped up, and . . . well, you already heard my other symptoms.*

Love is a funny thing. So are crushes—and that's what I had. A crush is an interest in a particular guy you're suddenly thinking about an awful lot. You find yourself doodling his name on your notebook, staring at him across the cafeteria, giggling when he talks to you (even though you're trying to be supercool), and somehow always ending up outside the gym when he's done with basketball practice.

You can develop a crush on a good guy friend you've known for ages or someone you've never talked to. Some adults call it

---

* To find out more about that first meeting with Mitch, listen to "Green Eyes and Yellow Tulips," episode 463, album 36, *Danger Signals*.

being *infatuated*, which can be defined as "an intense but short-lived passion or admiration for someone."

Being "in like" with someone is the next stage of a relationship, because you really get to know him—like I did with Mitch. You hang out with him, have some pretty deep conversations, and see him at both his worst and his best. You know he has some flaws, but you still look at him a little starry-eyed.

Then there's love. Love comes with commitment. You know you could spend the rest of your life with that person. Even if he was in a horrible accident and bound to a wheelchair, you'd still spend the rest of your days caring for him because of your deep love.

Most girls your age don't fall in love. It's something that happens as you get to know yourself better and have a greater maturity. Love isn't as much of a feeling as it is a choice and commitment to someone that develops out of feelings.

What Is Love . . .

Love isn't how it's depicted in books, movies, or songs. Candlelight dinners, long walks on the beach, or dances in the palace give us warm and fuzzy feelings. But that's not relationship. That's romance.

Girls—of all ages—are sometimes deceived by the "happily ever after" idea of romance. We think if a guy loves us, then all our problems will go away. We'll never feel sad or lonely or inadequate. But that's not the truth. No guy in this world can fix your life—not even your future husband. The only Love (notice the capital *L*) that can fill your heart is Jesus Himself. He *is* love. To grow in understanding of what true love is, know Him, talk to Him, and learn more of who He created you to be.

But be warned: the path to finding your future husband can be filled with heartache. Every time we develop a crush or have a boyfriend, it opens up the possibility that we could hurt a piece of our hearts. Proverbs 4:23 tells us, "Guard your heart above all else, for it determines the course of your life" (NLT). Isn't that amazing? How you protect your heart impacts the course of your life!

God doesn't tell us this to keep us from experiencing long walks on the beach and fuzzy feelings, but because He wants to protect us from giving our hearts away too soon—and to the wrong guy. He loves us so much, He doesn't want to see us hurt over and over again.

When we start putting our identity and value into what a guy thinks of us, that's not healthy. And even if you get a guy to notice you, it's usually the case that his attention will soon move to another girl. Boys aren't ready for long-term love yet (and neither are you). God wants something better for us.

I wish I'd known this back when I was a teenager. I kissed a boy before I should have. I thought I was old enough—and I really liked him. We spent a lot of time together, and my heart was growing really attached. When we broke up, though, it was one of the most painful things I had ever experienced. (Even worse than being snubbed by my Snack Pack friends.) I let my heart get connected in a way I shouldn't have, and I realized it too late.*

Relating to boys and having healthy relationships with them is something every girl deals with. Here's what my friends said:

> Camilla: Boys gross me out. They make jokes all the time and laugh at things that aren't funny. Most of them smell like the sweaty soccer socks at the bottom of my locker. Really . . . what is their deal? I'd rather hang out with my girlfriends and talk about stuff we like.
>
> Tamika: A couple of boys in my class seem pretty nice. And they're kinda cute. I don't think about them a lot, but when I'm hanging out with my friends and someone asks about which guys I like, those are the ones I mention.
>
> Emily: Just a couple of weeks ago, I noticed a new boy in band class. There was something about him I was drawn to. I kept looking in his direction to see what he was doing. Later, when he asked me where the sheet music was, I fumbled over what to say. Instead of "in the top drawer of the file cabinet," I said, "in the flop core of the tile dabinet." He just looked at me all confused and left. Oops.
>
> Olivia: I'm noticing a lot of guys. Sometimes in algebra class, I'll stare out the window and think about a guy I'd really

---

* To find out more about Connie's early relationship with Jeff Lewis, listen to "First Love," episode 111, album 8, *Beyond Expectations.*

like to talk to. Sometimes I'll wait at my locker on purpose until a certain guy walks by so I can start a conversation about something—an upcoming soccer game or the strange tie the assistant principal is wearing. It's never a big deal, but I'll end up replaying the conversation over and over again and talking to my friends about it.

Right Versus Wrong Places

Girls entering their teen years can range from grossed out by guys to a little interested to boy-crazy. No matter where you see yourself on that scale, it's all normal. It doesn't mean someone is more grown up because she's more interested in boys. It's just the way we're each individually made. Sometimes girls make the mistake of thinking they're more mature if a boy likes them or they're "going out" with a boy. Trust me, none of those things brings you closer to being an adult. In fact, sometimes if we're excessively into guys, it can *hinder* our maturity.

If we become obsessed with guys, we might focus all our time and energy on them. Instead of working at school or developing our talents, we're obsessed with texting, talking, and daydreaming about a boy. So instead of growing into the young women God created us to be, we build our identities around what guys think of us. That's a bad idea and can cause us to miss out on cool opportunities. Just hear what happened to Olivia's friend.

Olivia's Story

My friend was a lot of fun, crazy smart, and an amazing singer. But she was also incredibly boy-crazy. She got it into her head that if a boy liked her, then she had to change her personality to be attractive to him. She found out that Cory—a guy she really liked—thought girls on the dance team were cool. So she quit choir, joined the dance team, and started wearing clothes she thought would get his attention. To be honest, she became a different person. She wanted to talk only about Cory—what he said, did, and wore. She didn't do the fun things she used to do because she was so concerned about what Cory would think. When he came around, she'd swoon over him. It was sad that she gave up singing just to impress him. What a waste.

Unfortunately, Olivia's friend's story is pretty common. Girls who struggle with their self-esteem often think that the affection of a guy will make them feel more valuable. They crave male attention—even at the cost of losing who they're really meant to be. They might get an occasional rush of happiness when the guy gives them some time, but that's surrounded by a lot of uncertainty, fakeness, and desperation.

> ## Here's a Secret...
>
> A girl who's involved in activities and develops the confidence that trying new things builds is *way* more attractive to guys than a girl who just follows boys around giggling. Not that you should join an activity to catch a guy's eye (do it for you!). But as you get older, you'll see that the girls who know who they are and have confidence in their abilities are the ones who have guys looking their way.

Girls who begin putting their identity into what boys think of them struggle with figuring out who they really are. Don't make that mistake. No guy is worth changing how you look, what you believe, or what you're interested in.

Although it might be fun to giggle about who's cute at a slumber party, you don't want to become part of the boring group of girls who obsess about boys. There's way more to life than that. Wait until you're ready emotionally and socially, and your parents give you the thumbs-up sign, before you think about dating or developing deeper relationships with boys. Now is the time to enjoy being the age you are and growing into who God created you to be. Don't let boys distract you from that adventure!

My friends had some ideas about what to do instead of becoming obsessed with guys:

CAMILLA: Join a sports team. You'll get in shape, learn to work as a group, and have a blast hanging out together. There's nothing like the rush of competition.

PENNY: Spend time building your female friendships. Now is your chance to enjoy being a girl. Laugh together, have deep conversations, try out different hairstyles on each other, go roller skating, take selfies, write a blog together.

EMILY: Study. I know, I know . . . boring. But if you focus on schoolwork now, it'll help you get into college later—and maybe even earn a scholarship! Check out books on subjects you're interested in: dolphin training, astronomy, or meteorology (so you could be a weather girl on the nightly news!) Learn now what you enjoy.

TAMIKA: Develop a hobby. Write a screenplay for a movie. Enter pictures in a photography contest. Try pottery. Audition for the solo in the spring concert. Organize volunteer projects for your youth group. The possibilities are endless for clubs and activities to be involved in—take advantage of them!

OLIVIA: Plan fun activities with your family. A weekend road trip, a backyard camping adventure, or a homemade Japanese dinner (try using chopsticks) will make much better memories than, "Oh yeah, I followed a guy around the mall for an hour. I don't remember his name."

The Celebrity Crush

A few years ago, I accidentally won a date with a well-known actor, Chad Pearson.* A lot of girls in town had huge crushes on him, but I didn't understand why. What was so special about him besides all the cameras that followed him around? Pretty quickly, I found out he was just a normal guy. He had insecurities, he made mistakes, and he even had annoying habits—like always wanting to talk about himself. *Blah.* The girls in town were head over heels about the Chad Pearson that the media portrayed on the red carpet, but they had no idea who he really was.

You might have a friend who has posters and paraphernalia all over her room that feature her favorite guy singer or actor. She probably knows all the facts about him: birthday, favorite color, shoe size, hair-gel preference. But she doesn't really *know* him. Crushes like this can be pretty safe. We don't have to worry about being disappointed by our crush or being put in an awkward situ-

---

* To hear all about this date, listen to "This Is Chad Pearson?," episode 220, album 16, *Flights of Imagination.*

ation, because we'll likely never meet the guy. That said, celebrity crushes can go too far if they distract you from what's going on in the real world—or if you start boring your friends to death.

A Puzzling Situation . . .

Penny, Wooton, and I were putting together a puzzle of a dog wearing a Christmas sweater. (Don't ask . . . it was Wooton's puzzle.) We were about halfway through when Wooton found a puzzle piece under the table. He felt sorry for the neglected piece. From that point on, he was determined to find its place in the puzzle. While Penny and I put together the rest of the puzzle, he tried unsuccessfully to put that piece where it belonged. When we finished, there was still no place for it.

"Oh!" Wooton realized. "This is from the kitten-wearing-fairy-wings puzzle we put together last week!"

Having a boyfriend as a young teen is kind of like putting kitten fairy wings into a doggie Christmas puzzle. It doesn't fit! God's still showing you how to connect with Him. He's revealing your heart, gifts, and beauty. You don't know yet what kind of guy will be a good fit for your life. Besides, if you try to jam cats and dogs together, it creates a lot of drama and fighting. And when teens get deeply romantically involved too soon, that's exactly what can happen. . . . Well, minus some of the barking and scratching.

Maybe you can't help but notice that cute guy in your class, but it doesn't mean you have to center your life around him. You have too much going for you to do that! So rest assured that you haven't contracted mad cow disease and, for the time being, just enjoy getting to know your friends, yourself, and the God who has your steps planned out (Proverbs 16:9).

Your Turn

God created girls to be attracted to boys and made guys to notice girls. But relationships can be tricky—and not just at your age. Sometimes it's easier to give advice than take it. So think of a friend you have (or a little sister) who's a few years younger than you. What advice would you give her about boys?

_____

_____

Now go back and read your advice. Do you see some wisdom in it? How can you follow your best advice?

_____

_____

_____

Chapter 11

A Knight in Shining Arrogance

(How to Spot a Godly Guy)

My friend Joanne Allen told me that when she was in college, the quarterback of the football team asked her out. She was thrilled. All the girls were crazy about him. He drove a motorcycle, was really handsome, wore a leather jacket, and had just led their football team to a conference championship. He was the BMOC—big man on campus! (That's what they called the most popular guys back then.)

When he asked Joanne out, she accepted immediately. But

only an hour into their date, he proved less than impressive. Although this guy looked great from the outside, he was rude to the server who brought them their pizza, didn't open the door for Joanne, made fun of a man with physical disabilities, and spent the entire date bragging about himself. He never even asked Joanne a single question about *her* life.

"He might have been the BMOC," she told me, "but he was more like a BDOC—big dud on campus."

Even if you're not dating or that interested in boys yet, it doesn't mean you can't start thinking about the qualities you appreciate about the guys in your life. What kind of guy would you eventually like to marry?

Since Katrina has the most experience with being married, let's hear from her about how she knew Eugene was the right guy.

Katrina's Story

Well, it took me awhile to know for certain. Eugene isn't without his faults. He can overanalyze things and has been known to overreact. But I came to the point where I didn't doubt one bit that—while he wasn't perfect—he was the perfect man for *me*.

It began with our similarities. We both appreciated intellectual pursuits, discussing fine literature, and traveling. Though neither of us was a Christian when we first met, we were both seeking the truth and a deeper meaning in life. Connie helped me begin my relationship with Jesus Christ. After I made that decision,* it became more and more clear that I needed to make the hard decision to break up with Eugene. I knew that I couldn't be with someone who wasn't committed to following God.** I put off the decision because I loved Eugene, but I knew it was the right thing to do and I finally did it. When Eugene finally accepted Christ,*** I saw we were both dedicated to growing spiritually and putting God first. That's when we started dating again. I knew that I could trust Eugene to do what was best for our relationship, because he wanted to obey God. I respected that immensely.

I also saw characteristics in him that I appreciated.

---

* Katrina becomes a Christian in "It Ended with a Handshake," episode 267, album 20, *A Journey of Choices*.
** Katrina breaks up with Eugene in "The Turning Point," episode, 322, album 24, *Risks and Rewards*.
*** Want to find out why Eugene became a Christian? Listen to "The Time Has Come," episode 330, album 25, *Darkness Before Dawn*.

When he nursed me back to health after my face needed stitches, I could tell that he was caring and compassionate.* I also saw firsthand that he was a hard worker. Once he set his mind to something, he wouldn't give up. He also had a curiosity and thoughtfulness I greatly admired.

In addition to all these qualities that I valued were the things I felt in my heart. I don't rely completely on my heart for making decisions, as I know following our emotions without thinking logically can lead us down troublesome paths. But how I *felt* around Eugene was important too. He made me feel valuable and special. He never talked down to me but treated me with respect and listened intently to what I had to say. In his company, I always felt important, heard, and . . . lovely.

Katrina pointed out some really important aspects about finding quality guys (although if you'd told me a few years back that I'd be saying that about Eugene, I'd have thought you were crazy!). A shared faith, common interests, godly character qualities, and a heart attraction are all key ingredients for a lasting relationship.

Let's start with a shared faith. I learned this one the hard way when I first met Jeff Lewis, who I call my "first love"—because

---

* For the whole story, listen to "For Whom the Wedding Bells Toll, parts 1–3," episodes 372–374, album 29, *Signed, Sealed, and Committed.*

"first infatuation" doesn't look right in a scrapbook. Jeff was a great baseball player, shared my love for Mack Mason paraphernalia, and was a quality guy. My mom even called him "adorable." But he wasn't a Christian. I made excuses for a while: "He's such a great guy," "He's thinking about coming to church with me," and "We talk about Christianity—maybe this is how he'll become a Christian." But I knew deep down it was wrong. The Bible says, "Do not be unequally yoked with unbelievers" (2 Corinthians 6:14, ESV). Jeff was drawing me away from God, not closer to Him. And when God is the most important person in your life, you need Him to be most important to the guy you're dating too.

Love and romance matter to God. After all, He invented love. God gave us romantic feelings. He handcrafted the beauty of sunsets, roses, and candlelight. He knows what He's doing in the love department. Love is all over the Bible. I swoon every time I hear how Boaz cared for Ruth. I get misty-eyed when I imagine Isaac running to Rebekah. And did you know that Jacob loved Rachel so much, he worked seven years for her and "they seemed to him but a few days because of the love he had for her"? (Genesis 29:20, ESV).

In fact, at its core, the Bible is one big love letter to us. God loves us so much that He sent His Son to die for us. God understands that love takes patience, sacrifice, perseverance, and forgiveness. All that means we can trust Him completely when it comes to our future love lives. He knows the kind of guys who will help us grow closer to Him, who will help us use the gifts He's bestowed on us, and who will journey through life with us. God knows way better than even we do what's best for us . . . and the best timing for us to get into a serious relationship. So even though you're not nearly ready to get married, isn't it comforting that you can put this area of your life safely in God's hands and rely on Him for guidance? Yay, God!

Don't Let Your Eyes Deceive You

But sometimes we can get ahead of God or get distracted by things that aren't so important in His eyes. The outside parts of a guy—how he looks, how cool he seems—are usually the first things we notice. That's okay. It's natural to be drawn to a guy's appearance. But it shouldn't be the only thing we notice. Good looks fade and hair falls out, but the truly important thing doesn't change. And that's a guy's character.

Galatians 5:22-23 lists several godly characteristics. They're better known as the fruit of the Spirit, because you'll see these qualities in someone who's living for the Lord. Think of guys who interest you through the lens of these qualities: love, joy, peace, patience, kindness, goodness, faithfulness, gentleness, and self-control. Ask yourself, *Does he lose his temper? Is he rude to teachers?*

Does he make fun of kids? Does he shove into the front of the line in the cafeteria? Does he work hard in school? How kind is he to younger kids?

The answers to these questions will tell you a lot more about a guy's character than finding out what his batting average is or how many girls like him.

Another great exercise is looking around at how some of the godly men in your life treat women. The girls made the following observations:

TAMIKA: I notice how Jack Allen always talks so highly about his wife. Even when she's not around, he's always saying how wonderful she is.

OLIVIA: My dad always opens the door for my mom. And he'll bring her flowers on random occasions, like the first Monday in December or the anniversary of when they first held hands. I pretend to gag because, hey, they're my parents. But if I'm being honest, it's pretty sweet.

PENNY: My grandpa will settle Grandma on the couch with a glass of prune juice and trim her toenails every Friday night. Talk about romantic.

CAMILLA: My uncle loves to do practical things to help my aunt. He'll surprise her by folding the laundry or making dinner while she's out running errands.

EMILY: My dad leaves notes for my mom on the bathroom mirror about how much he loves her. She gets all glowy-looking after she reads them.

Your Turn

Some girls waste a lot of time and suffer a lot of heartbreak in their quest for a knight in shining armor. Because under that shiny exterior, some guys lack luster. Instead of falling for a good-looking package or some smooth talk, know what you're really looking for by putting a check mark next to the qualities below that you most want in your future husband. Mark just ten items and then go back and rank them in importance from 1 to 10, with 1 being the most important:

- ❏ Is funny
- ❏ Loves God
- ❏ Treats his mom nicely
- ❏ Has a great smile
- ❏ Is strong
- ❏ Works hard
- ❏ Acts intelligently
- ❏ Dresses well
- ❏ Is musical
- ❏ Is athletic

- ❏ Has confidence
- ❏ Is trustworthy and honest
- ❏ Controls his temper
- ❏ Shows affection
- ❏ Has a positive attitude
- ❏ Is a good listener
- ❏ Takes risks
- ❏ Is romantic
- ❏ Is loyal
- ❏ Helps others

When you're done, write down your picks for the top-ten characteristics in your notebook. Then refer back to this list when someone catches your eye so you can make sure you're looking at the right things.

The Big Deal About Dignity

Now that you're figuring out which qualities you're looking for most in a boy, it's also important to make a decision about certain *deal breakers* that would end a relationship or stop it before it starts. One of those is this: If a guy doesn't love and follow the Lord, don't consider him. A second deal breaker is lack of respect. Only date a guy who treats you with dignity. You can add other deal breakers to your list, but being treated with respect is a must-have for every girl. Katrina learned that the hard way.

Katrina's Story

After I graduated from college, I dated a guy who didn't really respect me. He'd make fun of me when we were with his friends and told me I should lose weight. But I thought, *Well, at least he's dating me.* I tried so hard to make the relationship work because I thought that was the loving thing to do. I didn't know Jesus then, so I didn't know what real love looked like. I didn't realize how messed up that thinking was until after he broke up with me. I now know that I deserve respect from a guy, and Eugene definitely gives me that.

Decide now to avoid guys who pressure you to go too far physically, want you to change and become someone you're not, or are critical of how you look. This isn't being treated with dignity. God wants better for you. Look for guys who honor you, support you, and bring out your best qualities.

And here's some good news: You can start enjoying friendships with guys right now. There are probably guys at your church or next to you in class who could make good friends. It's best to hang out in groups so you can practice looking for those qualities which may be hidden underneath their armor.

Friendship is a great way to get to know guys without the pressure of who likes who or the drama of breaking up. Friendships are fun, help you learn new things about yourself, and introduce you to interesting people.

I've appreciated my friendships with Wooton, Eugene, and Jason. Guys and girls often have different perspectives on things, so it's helped me to hear their thoughts. And they appreciate my input on what's going on in their lives too. (Well . . . usually.)

When to Start Dating

Every family has different ideas about this issue. The only right answer is the one that's right for you and your parents. Some families believe in courting (spending time together only with other people present, and with the intention of the relationship resulting in marriage) as opposed to dating.

Parents usually have an age in mind when their kids can start dating. Other parents wait to see how their kids are growing up and base it on when they feel each of them is mature enough. I've met great families who believe it's important to save your first kiss until your wedding day, or at least until you're engaged.

Other families think it's okay to kiss someone you've been dating or courting for a long time. There is no across-the-board, perfect answer for everybody.

Talk to your parents about their thoughts. Ask them when they started dating—and if they wished they'd started sooner or waited longer. Then find out what kind of boundaries they'd like you to set in your guy-girl relationship when that time comes. Wait to grow up a little more, and actually enjoy getting to know guys right now as just friends.

Here's a Secret...

Some kids "go out" in junior high, but it's really more about liking the idea of being liked. For some girls, it makes them feel grown up. But far from being grown up, these relationships are usually packed with immature drama. A girl may gossip to her friends, trying to figure out if a boy still likes her. Rumors often fly around about what the girl and boy do. Breakups occur through a friend or even a text message. Then the boy and girl feel awkward around each other after the breakup. Seriously, *avoid the drama*. Wait to grow up a little more, and actually *enjoy* getting to know a guy.

Chapter 12

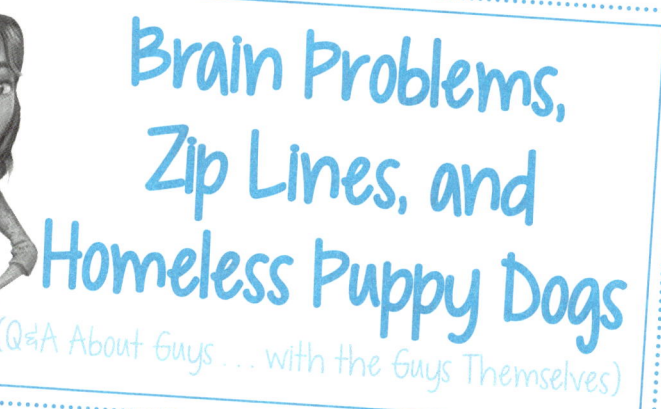

Brain Problems, Zip Lines, and Homeless Puppy Dogs
(Q&A About Guys... with the Guys Themselves)

I have a surprise for you! So close your eyes. Wait... you can't read with your eyes closed. Open your eyes.

Ta-da! Eugene, Jason, and Wooton finally decided where to put the new picnic table. Well, they didn't really decide, but they decided to let Whit decide. *Sigh*... men! But that's not the exciting part. This is: they agreed to answer some of the pressing questions we girls always wanted to ask about guys. So here we go. Since Camilla's the youngest, she went first.

CAMILLA: I have a friend who acts really strange around boys. She laughs *really* loud at some pretty stupid jokes and pretends she doesn't know things that she really does. Is this the kind of thing that attracts boys?

JASON: Yes . . . and no. Like everyone, guys like to think they're funny and smart. So your friend is probably feeding their egos by the way she acts. While she might get a guy's attention for a short time, she won't keep it. The thing with girls who act this way is that they're easily replaced. But a girl who's smart, interesting, and talented? *Whoa.* She might intimidate us at first, but in the long run, she'll earn more than just our attention. She'll get our respect and admiration as well.

WOOTON: Sometimes girls try to get you to like them by pretending to like the same things as you. Like if I say, "Wow! I really love licorice dipped in caramel with chocolate sprinkles," and she says, "Really? *I* love licorice dipped in caramel with chocolate sprinkles too!" then I start to think. First, I wonder if she's really being honest. And second it makes me think, *That's kinda boring.* I mean, I don't need a female version of me. Sure, I hope that I have things in common with whoever I marry. It would be great if she enjoys playing board games, hanging out with lots of people, and teaching a fifth-grade Sunday school class together. But I'd want her to have her own interests, thoughts, and ideas. Because if I want to hang out with someone just like me all the time, I can. And I already do that when I'm alone.

> ### Here's a Secret...
>
> Guys have problems with their brains. Well, kind of. See, girls' brains develop sooner than guys' brains. So as young teenagers, girls are generally more mature than guys of the same age. It's easier for girls to reason, remember, and focus in a classroom.[1] So if a guy likes you, he may push you, tease you, try to trip you, or throw things at you. Don't worry. His brain and maturity will develop. Give him time.

I was going to have Tamika go next, but Katrina jumped in with this question:

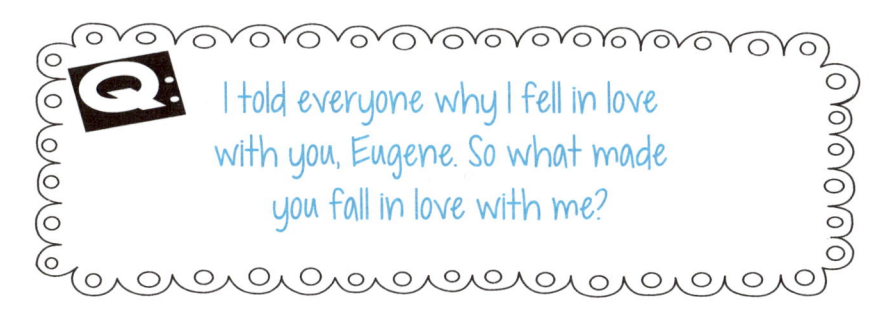

Q: I told everyone why I fell in love with you, Eugene. So what made you fall in love with me?

EUGENE: As you're aware, Katrina, when we first met, I honestly didn't pay much attention to you. I was more interested in a book that I needed. You happened to be the librarian who assisted me. But—I'll admit—it took only mere minutes for me to grow interested. We began discussing authors we both enjoyed, and I felt like I'd met a kindred spirit of sorts. The more time I spent with you, I realized you had a kind heart, a curious mind, and a sharp intellect—and I became quite smitten.*

But then you left Odyssey. And your absence truly did make my heart grow fonder. So once I accepted Christ, it became paramount to rekindle our relationship. From there, it didn't take long for me to honestly tell you that I believed Katrina Shanks to be the most beautiful woman I'd ever seen. Of course, now I would say that about Katrina *Meltsner*. You are stunning in every way.

Okay . . . okay. Enough gush, Eugene. *Blech*. And that gave Tamika her chance.

TAMIKA: What about you other guys? What do you think makes a girl attractive?

WOOTON: A girl with her own sense of style. Y'know, someone's who's confident in who she is. If she likes polka-dot

---

* For more of the Eugene and Katrina love story, listen to "Truth, Trivia, and 'Trina," episode 254, album 19, *Passport to Adventure*.

socks, she wears them. The kind of girl that people like being around, because she's warm and friendly and starts conversations. It's easier to approach a girl who smiles a lot. Not just at you but at everyone. Cute girls might turn our heads, but if we're looking for someone to really get to know, we want someone who's more than a pretty face. She has to know who she is and not be afraid of standing out. By the way, a girl who constantly whines, gossips, and criticizes others is a big turnoff.

JASON: It's nice when a girl asks you about your life—the score of your baseball game or how your latest secret-agent mission went. Well, that might just be me. I get really annoyed when a girl is too concerned about her appearance. I mean, really, how are you supposed to zip line across a rain forest without getting your hair messed up? Just have fun being friends with guys and be willing to be adventurous.

I've certainly been on my share of adventures with Jason. It seems like intrigue follows him everywhere. Speaking of intriguing, here's Olivia's question:

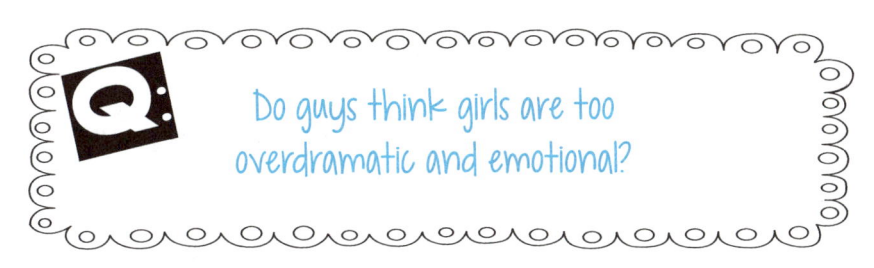

Q: Do guys think girls are too overdramatic and emotional?

EUGENE: Indubitably. But the male of the species must realize this is *not* a flaw. Girls often display a full array of emotions for all to see. Guys temper their true feelings. But emotions are God-given. Do not think for one moment that we lack emotion. We have the same feelings as girls. We may feel inadequate, embarrassed, or bullied. But guys have been taught by their fathers and society to be tough and stoic. Under a hard shell, many guys are—how can I put this?—squishy. Here's Wooton's unique take:

Wooton's Story

With all of this question asking and answering, it reminded me of a question I've always wanted to ask. This has confused me for years. I mean, when I lived in Alaska, I understood why wolves hunted in packs. But I've never known why girls go to the bathroom in groups. So why is it? And I hope it's not so you can prey on the weak and the old, like the wolves do.

OLIVIA: It's so we can share lip gloss.

PENNY: We use that time to check in with each other and ask each other questions like, "Are you doing okay?" "Do you want to leave?" and "Is he annoying you?" Y'know, all the conversations we can't have in front of you.

EMILY: In public places like the mall or movies, it's just safer.

TAMIKA: So we can laugh really loud together at something that just happened.

CAMILLA: Because we know it drives you crazy wondering what we're talking about.

Emily was up next. Here's what she asked:

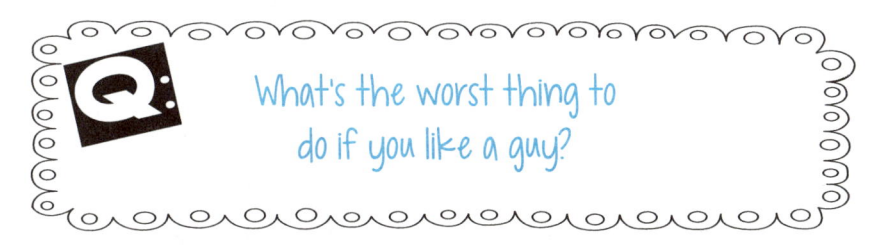

Q: What's the worst thing to do if you like a guy?

WOOTON: Follow him around like a homeless puppy dog. A girl who acts like that seems like she has nothing else interesting in her life. And don't act like a kitty cat either. If you lick the back of your hands in front of us and arch your back a lot, it just seems weird. Really, acting like any animal around a guy is just a bad idea.

JASON: Tell all your friends . . . and his friends. There's nothing more embarrassing than having a bunch of girls giggling when you pass by, handing you notes, or coming up to you in front of your friends and saying, "Do you like so-and-so? She thinks you're *sooooo* cute." If you want to get to know a guy a little better, let him know face-to-face. It shows you have confidence and are worth getting to know. But don't be too forward. Guys still like to be the ones who are doing the pursuing.

Penny had a dreamy question:

> **Q:** I had a dream about a guy. Does that mean I like him?

WOOTON: Uh, no. Unless it was about . . . Never mind. If dreams about people meant that we liked them, it would mean I've had crushes on my second-grade Sunday school teacher (who was ninety-seven), the girl dressed up like a slice of pizza handing out flyers, and the Swiss Miss cocoa girl. And I guess I might have been in love with the pizza or wanted some hot cocoa, but I wasn't interested in the girls in the dreams I had.

Thinking someone is attractive or being fascinated by how a skateboarder can do all those cool tricks doesn't mean you have a crush on him. Don't overthink it. I know I never do.

All of these answers had been very enlightening, but we were out of food, and I was getting ants all over me. So we called this picnic over. But before we left, I had one last question:

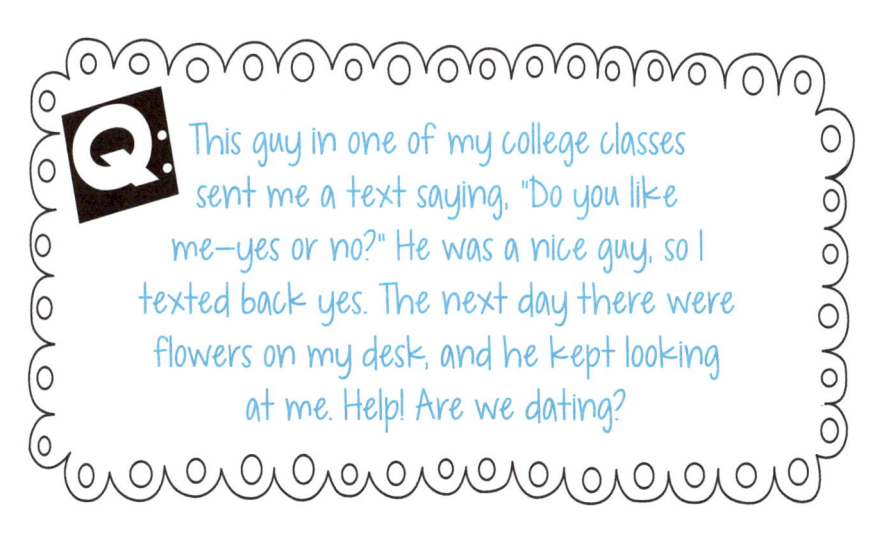

> **Q:** This guy in one of my college classes sent me a text saying, "Do you like me—yes or no?" He was a nice guy, so I texted back yes. The next day there were flowers on my desk, and he kept looking at me. Help! Are we dating?

EUGENE: Ah . . . yes, a classic misunderstanding. "Like" can mean a multitude of things. I like my friends. I like cheeseburgers with extra pickles. And I like experimenting with non-Newtonian fluids. The best thing you can do, Miss Kendall, is have a sit-down conversation with this young man. Tell him that even though you like him, you don't mean in the romantic sense. Your feelings are more platonic. While he may be hurt at first, he'll appreciate your being forthright.

JASON: The worst thing you can do is humiliate a guy. We might act tough, but our feelings get hurt too. So don't post on Facebook about how he sent you flowers, but you don't like him. As a rule, respect guys just like you'd want to be respected. Even if you might be worried about hurting a guy's feelings by turning him down, it's always better to be honest up front.

Well, thanks for joining with my friends and me! I hope you enjoyed the conversation. And I *really* hope you have a better idea of how to journey through the next few years. By having a good idea of who you are and how God sees you, you can stand strong when faced with cliques, peer pressure, and the emotions that come along with guys. Rough spots will come, but I know God has a great calling on your life. And He'll be with you every step of the way!

Oh . . . and one more thing, most people prefer pickle relish in their egg-salad sandwiches. Go figure.

Your Turn

Take a few minutes for reflection. What did you learn about guys from Jason, Wooton, and Eugene? Did any of the questions remind you of situations you or your friends have faced with guys? If so, how?

Now that you've finished this book, what are some things you learned? Write a letter to your future self. Remind the "future you" about what's important to you, how you want your teen years to look, what you value, and the kinds of friends (girls and guys) you want in your life.

Appendix

(Verses About How God Sees You)

If you feel like giving up, remember Romans 8:37: "No, in all these things we are more than conquerors through him who loved us."

If you feel like you don't matter, remember Philippians 2:15, (2011): "You will shine among them like stars in the sky."

If you feel lonely, remember Hebrews 13:5: "God has said, 'Never will I leave you; never will I forsake you.'"

If you feel unimportant, remember 1 Peter 2:9, (2011): "But you are a chosen people, a royal priesthood, a holy nation, God's special possession."

If you feel that you're ugly, remember Ephesians 2:10, NLT: "We are God's masterpiece. He has created us anew in Christ Jesus." And also Psalm 139:14: "I praise you because I am fearfully and wonderfully made; your works are wonderful, I know that full well."

If you feel you've made too many mistakes, remember 2 Corinthians 5:17: "Therefore, if anyone is in Christ, he is a new creation; the old has gone, the new has come!"

If you feel that you're forgotten, remember John 15:16: "You did not choose me, but I chose you and appointed you to go and bear fruit."

If you feel unlovable, remember 1 John 3:1: "How great is the love the Father has lavished on us, that we should be called children of God! And that is what we are!" And Zephaniah 3:17, NLT: "The LORD your God is living among you. He is a mighty savior. He will take delight in you with gladness. With his love, he will calm all your fears. He will rejoice over you with joyful songs."

If you feel hopeless, remember Jeremiah 29:11: " 'For I know the plans I have for you,' declares the LORD, 'plans to prosper you and not to harm you, plans to give you hope and a future.' "

If you feel sad or discouraged, remember 1 Peter 5:7, NLT: "Give all your worries and cares to God, because he cares about you."

If you feel like your life was a mistake, remember Jeremiah 1:5: "Before I formed you in the womb I knew you, before you were born I set you apart."

If you feel unnoticed, remember Matthew 10:29-31, NLT: "What is the price of two sparrows—one copper coin? But not a single sparrow can fall to the ground without your Father knowing it. And the very hairs on your head are all numbered. So don't be afraid; you are more valuable to God than a whole flock of sparrows."

Notes

Chapter 6
1. From Margaret Blackstone and Elissa Haddon Guest, *Girl Stuff: A Survival Guide to Growing Up* (Orlando: Harcourt, 2000).
2. Rana Sampson, "Bullying in Schools," Guide No. 12, 2002, Center for Problem-Oriented Policing, http://www.popcenter.org/problems/bullying/1.
3. US Department of Education, National Center for Education Statistics, "Student Reports of Bullying and Cyber-Bullying: Results From the 2011 School Crime Supplement to the National Crime Victimization Survey," August 2013, http://nces.ed.gov/pubs2013/2013329.pdf, page T3, table 2.1

Chapter 8
1. Eric H. Chudler, "Neuroscience for Kids: Brain Development," University of Washington, 2012, https://faculty.washington.edu/chudler/dev.html.
2. Cited in Arthur Allen, "Risky Behavior by Teens Can Be Explained in Part by How Their Brains Change," *Washington Post,* September 1, 2014, http://www.washingtonpost.com/national/health-science/risky-behavior-by-teens-can-be-explained-in-part-by-how-their-brains-change/2014/08/29/28405df0-27d2-11e4-8593-da634b334390_story.html.
3. Thomas R. Frieden, foreword to *Preventing Tobacco Use Among Youth and Young Adults: A Report of the Surgeon General* (Atlanta: US Department of Health and Human Services, Centers for Disease Control and Prevention, 2012), http://www.surgeongeneral.gov/library/reports/preventing-youth-tobacco-use/full-report.pdf.
4. National Youth Tobacco survey data, 2011–2013, published in *Nicotine and Tobacco Research*, cited in "More Than a Quarter-Million Youth Who Had Never Smoked a Cigarette Used E-Cigarettes in 2013," CDC Newsroom, Centers for Disease Control and Prevention, August 25, 2014, http://www.cdc.gov/media/releases/2014/p0825-e-cigarettes.html.

5. Studies cited in "Smoking and Tobacco Use: Health Effects of Cigarette Smoking," Fact Sheets, Centers for Disease Control and Prevention, accessed February 6, 2014, http://www.cdc.gov/tobacco/data_statistics/fact_sheets/health_effects/effects_cig_smoking.
6. Study by Johns Hopkins School of Public Health, published in *Journal of Addictive Diseases*, cited in "Is Smoking a Gateway Drug?" Teen Smoking, accessed December 20, 2014, http://www.teensmoking.us/content/is-smoking-a-gateway-drug.html.

Chapter 12
1. Michael Gurian, *The Purpose of Boys* (San Francisco: Jossey-Bass, 2009), 161.